TEACHER'S PET PUBLICATIONS

PUZZLE PACK
for
Go Ask Alice

based on the anonymous diary of a teenage girl

Written by
Mary B. Collins

© 2008 Teacher's Pet Publications
All Rights Reserved

The materials in this packet are copyrighted
by Teacher's Pet Publications, Inc.

These pages may be duplicated by the purchaser
for use in the purchaser's own classroom.

Copying any of these materials and distributing them
for any other purpose is a violation of the copyright laws.

© 2008 Teacher's Pet Publications, Inc.
www.tpet.com

INTRODUCTION
If you already own the LitPlan for this title, this Puzzle Pack will refresh your Unit Resource Materials and Vocabulary Resource Materials sections plus give you additional materials you can substitute into the tests. If you do not already have a complete LitPlan, these pages will give you some supplemental materials to use with your own plan. There are two main groups of materials: one set for unit words (such as characters' names, symbols, places, etc.) and one set for vocabulary words associated with the book.

WORD LIST
There is a word list for both the unit words and the vocabulary words. These lists show you which words are being used in the materials and the clues or definitions being used for those words. You may want to give students a word list with clues/definitions to help them, or you may want students to only have a word list (without clues/definitions) if you want them to work a little harder. Both are available for duplication. The word lists can also be your "calling key" for the bingo games.

FILL IN THE BLANK AND MATCHING
There are 4 each of the fill in the blank and matching worksheets for both the unit and vocabulary words. These pages can be used either as extra worksheets for students or as objective parts of a unit test. They can be done individually if students need extra help or as a whole class activity to review the material covered.

MAGIC SQUARES
The magic squares not only reinforce the material covered but also work on reasoning and math skills. Many teachers have told us that their students really enjoy doing these!

WORD SEARCH PUZZLES
The word search words go in all directions, as indicated on your answer keys. Two of the word search puzzles have the clues listed rather than the words. This makes the puzzle a little more difficult, but it reinforces the material better. Two word search puzzles have words only for students who find the clue puzzles too difficult.

CROSSWORD PUZZLES
Both unit and vocabulary word sections have 4 crossword puzzles.

BINGO CARDS
There are 32 individual bingo cards for the unit words and 32 individual bingo cards for the vocabulary words. You can use your word list as a "call list," calling the words at random and marking them off of your list as you go, or you could use the flash cards by cutting them apart and drawing the words at random from a hat (or box or whatever). To make a better review, you might ask for the definition and spelling of each word as you call it out–or you could call out the definitions and have students tell you the words they need to look for on the puzzle.

JUGGLE LETTERS
The vocabulary juggle letter game is intended to help students learn the spellings of the words. One sheet has the definitions listed on it as an extra help for students who need it or to reinforce the definitions if you choose to do so.

FLASH CARDS
We've included a set of vocabulary flash cards you can duplicate, cut, and fold for your students. Some teachers make a few sets for general use by the class; others make a set for each student. Some teachers duplicate them for each student and have the students cut & fold their own. You can cut out just the words and put them in a hat, have each student pick out one word and write the definition and a sentence for that word. Students then swap words and papers, with the next student adding a sentence of his own under the last one. You can have students swap as many times as you like. Each time the student will read the sentences written prior to his own and then add a sentence. You can cut out the words and definitions separately and play "I Have; Who Has?" Each student in the room draws a word and definition. The first student says, "I have (the name of the word). Who has the definition?" The student with the definition reads it then says, "I have (the name of the vocabulary word she has). Who has the definition?" The round continues until all words and definitions have been given.

Go Ask Alice Word List

No.	Word	Clue/Definition
1.	ALEX	Alice's younger sister
2.	ALICE	She wrote the diary and died.
3.	BABBIE	Girl in mental hospital whose parents decide to give her up to foster care
4.	BOUTIQUE	Kind of store Alice and Chris open
5.	CANDY	What Alice wants to put drugs on to get her younger brother to experience being high
6.	CAR	Kids at school threaten to hide drugs in Alice's father's ___ to get him in trouble.
7.	CHICAGO	City where Joel lives
8.	CHRIS	Girl Alice runs away with
9.	CHRISTMAS	Alice's favorite holiday
10.	CLEANING	Alice has fun doing this with her family after a New Year's Eve party.
11.	DENVER	City Alice first goes to the second time she runs away
12.	DIARY	What Alice locks in a metal box
13.	DINNER	Alice makes this for her mother as a surprise for her birthday.
14.	ELEMENTARY	Alice is ashamed that she sells drugs at the ___ school.
15.	FAWN	'Straight' girl Alice becomes friends with
16.	GRANDMA	Alice stays to help her around the house over the summer.
17.	GRANDPA	He has a heart attack and dies.
18.	HAPPINESS	Kitten belonging to Alice's sister; makes Alice appreciate the pleasures of life without drugs
19.	JAN	Girl who shows up high while Alice is babysitting
20.	JEWELRY	While in San Francisco, Alice works at a shop that sells this.
21.	JILL	Girl's house where Alice played 'Button, Button, Who's Got the Button?'
22.	JOEL	Boy Alice meets at the university library; he is supportive
23.	LARSEN	Last name of the family Alice babysits for
24.	LETTER	Joel sends Alice this while she is in the hospital.
25.	LSD	Drug in Alice's Coke when she first took drugs
26.	MARCIE	Girl who lies to the judge and gets Alice sent to a mental hospital
27.	MISSION	People who take Alice to the doctor & give her food & clothes
28.	MOUNTAINS	Place Alice's parents take Chris and Alice for a fun weekend away from the kids at school
29.	PEANUTS	They were covered in acid, sending Alice on a bad trip ending with her going to the hospital.
30.	PIANO	Instrument Alice plays
31.	PREGNANT	Because Alice is worried she is ___, she can't sleep, and the doctor prescribes tranquilizers.
32.	PROFESSOR	The job of Alice's father
33.	RICHIE	Name of boyfriend who got Alice into selling drugs
34.	ROGER	Boy Alice really likes; he stands her up at the start of the book
35.	SHELIA	Chris's employer; turns the girls onto drugs in San Francisco
36.	TIM	Alice's younger brother

Go Ask Alice Fill In The Blanks 1

_____

_____

_____

_____

_____

_____

_____

_____

_____

_____

_____

_____

_____

_____

_____

_____

_____

_____

_____

_____

1. Place Alice's parents take Chris and Alice for a fun weekend away from the kids at school
2. Last name of the family Alice babysits for
3. Girl Alice runs away with
4. Alice has fun doing this with her family after a New Year's Eve party.
5. Alice's younger sister
6. Girl's house where Alice played 'Button, Button, Who's Got the Button?'
7. She wrote the diary and died.
8. Alice stays to help her around the house over the summer.
9. Drug in Alice's Coke when she first took drugs
10. Joel sends Alice this while she is in the hospital.
11. What Alice locks in a metal box
12. He has a heart attack and dies.
13. Alice makes this for her mother as a surprise for her birthday.
14. Chris's employer; turns the girls onto drugs in San Francisco
15. Name of boyfriend who got Alice into selling drugs
16. They were covered in acid, sending Alice on a bad trip ending with her going to the hospital.
17. City where Joel lives
18. Girl who lies to the judge and gets Alice sent to a mental hospital
19. Girl who shows up high while Alice is babysitting
20. Because Alice is worried she is ___, she can't sleep, and the doctor prescribes tranquilizers.

Go Ask Alice Fill In The Blanks 1 Answer Key

MOUNTAINS	1. Place Alice's parents take Chris and Alice for a fun weekend away from the kids at school
LARSEN	2. Last name of the family Alice babysits for
CHRIS	3. Girl Alice runs away with
CLEANING	4. Alice has fun doing this with her family after a New Year's Eve party.
ALEX	5. Alice's younger sister
JILL	6. Girl's house where Alice played 'Button, Button, Who's Got the Button?'
ALICE	7. She wrote the diary and died.
GRANDMA	8. Alice stays to help her around the house over the summer.
LSD	9. Drug in Alice's Coke when she first took drugs
LETTER	10. Joel sends Alice this while she is in the hospital.
DIARY	11. What Alice locks in a metal box
GRANDPA	12. He has a heart attack and dies.
DINNER	13. Alice makes this for her mother as a surprise for her birthday.
SHELIA	14. Chris's employer; turns the girls onto drugs in San Francisco
RICHIE	15. Name of boyfriend who got Alice into selling drugs
PEANUTS	16. They were covered in acid, sending Alice on a bad trip ending with her going to the hospital.
CHICAGO	17. City where Joel lives
MARCIE	18. Girl who lies to the judge and gets Alice sent to a mental hospital
JAN	19. Girl who shows up high while Alice is babysitting
PREGNANT	20. Because Alice is worried she is ___, she can't sleep, and the doctor prescribes tranquilizers.

Go Ask Alice Fill In The Blanks 2

1. Girl's house where Alice played 'Button, Button, Who's Got the Button?'
2. Instrument Alice plays
3. 'Straight' girl Alice becomes friends with
4. Girl Alice runs away with
5. Kind of store Alice and Chris open
6. What Alice wants to put drugs on to get her younger brother to experience being high
7. City Alice first goes to the second time she runs away
8. Kitten belonging to Alice's sister; makes Alice appreciate the pleasures of life without drugs
9. Alice's younger sister
10. Boy Alice meets at the university library; he is supportive
11. What Alice locks in a metal box
12. Alice stays to help her around the house over the summer.
13. Last name of the family Alice babysits for
14. Chris's employer; turns the girls onto drugs in San Francisco
15. Name of boyfriend who got Alice into selling drugs
16. Joel sends Alice this while she is in the hospital.
17. They were covered in acid, sending Alice on a bad trip ending with her going to the hospital.
18. The job of Alice's father
19. Girl who lies to the judge and gets Alice sent to a mental hospital
20. Alice is ashamed that she sells drugs at the ___ school.

Go Ask Alice Fill In The Blanks 2 Answer Key

JILL	1. Girl's house where Alice played 'Button, Button, Who's Got the Button?'
PIANO	2. Instrument Alice plays
FAWN	3. 'Straight' girl Alice becomes friends with
CHRIS	4. Girl Alice runs away with
BOUTIQUE	5. Kind of store Alice and Chris open
CANDY	6. What Alice wants to put drugs on to get her younger brother to experience being high
DENVER	7. City Alice first goes to the second time she runs away
HAPPINESS	8. Kitten belonging to Alice's sister; makes Alice appreciate the pleasures of life without drugs
ALEX	9. Alice's younger sister
JOEL	10. Boy Alice meets at the university library; he is supportive
DIARY	11. What Alice locks in a metal box
GRANDMA	12. Alice stays to help her around the house over the summer.
LARSEN	13. Last name of the family Alice babysits for
SHELIA	14. Chris's employer; turns the girls onto drugs in San Francisco
RICHIE	15. Name of boyfriend who got Alice into selling drugs
LETTER	16. Joel sends Alice this while she is in the hospital.
PEANUTS	17. They were covered in acid, sending Alice on a bad trip ending with her going to the hospital.
PROFESSOR	18. The job of Alice's father
MARCIE	19. Girl who lies to the judge and gets Alice sent to a mental hospital
ELEMENTARY	20. Alice is ashamed that she sells drugs at the ___ school.

Go Ask Alice Fill In The Blanks 3

_____

_____

_____

_____

_____

_____

_____

_____

_____

_____

_____

_____

_____

_____

_____

_____

_____

_____

_____

_____

1. Alice has fun doing this with her family after a New Year's Eve party.
2. While in San Francisco, Alice works at a shop that sells this.
3. Alice is ashamed that she sells drugs at the ___ school.
4. He has a heart attack and dies.
5. Girl in mental hospital whose parents decide to give her up to foster care
6. Joel sends Alice this while she is in the hospital.
7. City where Joel lives
8. She wrote the diary and died.
9. Alice's younger sister
10. Kind of store Alice and Chris open
11. Boy Alice meets at the university library; he is supportive
12. Alice makes this for her mother as a surprise for her birthday.
13. Alice's favorite holiday
14. Alice's younger brother
15. Last name of the family Alice babysits for
16. Place Alice's parents take Chris and Alice for a fun weekend away from the kids at school
17. 'Straight' girl Alice becomes friends with
18. People who take Alice to the doctor & give her food & clothes
19. Because Alice is worried she is ___, she can't sleep, and the doctor prescribes tranquilizers.
20. Boy Alice really likes; he stands her up at the start of the book

Go Ask Alice Fill In The Blanks 3 Answer Key

CLEANING	1. Alice has fun doing this with her family after a New Year's Eve party.
JEWELRY	2. While in San Francisco, Alice works at a shop that sells this.
ELEMENTARY	3. Alice is ashamed that she sells drugs at the ___ school.
GRANDPA	4. He has a heart attack and dies.
BABBIE	5. Girl in mental hospital whose parents decide to give her up to foster care
LETTER	6. Joel sends Alice this while she is in the hospital.
CHICAGO	7. City where Joel lives
ALICE	8. She wrote the diary and died.
ALEX	9. Alice's younger sister
BOUTIQUE	10. Kind of store Alice and Chris open
JOEL	11. Boy Alice meets at the university library; he is supportive
DINNER	12. Alice makes this for her mother as a surprise for her birthday.
CHRISTMAS	13. Alice's favorite holiday
TIM	14. Alice's younger brother
LARSEN	15. Last name of the family Alice babysits for
MOUNTAINS	16. Place Alice's parents take Chris and Alice for a fun weekend away from the kids at school
FAWN	17. 'Straight' girl Alice becomes friends with
MISSION	18. People who take Alice to the doctor & give her food & clothes
PREGNANT	19. Because Alice is worried she is ___, she can't sleep, and the doctor prescribes tranquilizers.
ROGER	20. Boy Alice really likes; he stands her up at the start of the book

Go Ask Alice Fill In The Blanks 4

_____ 1. Chris's employer; turns the girls onto drugs in San Francisco

_____ 2. The job of Alice's father

_____ 3. Joel sends Alice this while she is in the hospital.

_____ 4. She wrote the diary and died.

_____ 5. 'Straight' girl Alice becomes friends with

_____ 6. They were covered in acid, sending Alice on a bad trip ending with her going to the hospital.

_____ 7. Girl in mental hospital whose parents decide to give her up to foster care

_____ 8. Girl who lies to the judge and gets Alice sent to a mental hospital

_____ 9. Kind of store Alice and Chris open

_____ 10. Alice's younger sister

_____ 11. Alice's younger brother

_____ 12. Alice's favorite holiday

_____ 13. Girl Alice runs away with

_____ 14. What Alice locks in a metal box

_____ 15. Kitten belonging to Alice's sister; makes Alice appreciate the pleasures of life without drugs

_____ 16. Alice makes this for her mother as a surprise for her birthday.

_____ 17. Boy Alice really likes; he stands her up at the start of the book

_____ 18. While in San Francisco, Alice works at a shop that sells this.

_____ 19. Girl who shows up high while Alice is babysitting

_____ 20. City where Joel lives

Go Ask Alice Fill In The Blanks 4 Answer Key

SHELIA	1. Chris's employer; turns the girls onto drugs in San Francisco
PROFESSOR	2. The job of Alice's father
LETTER	3. Joel sends Alice this while she is in the hospital.
ALICE	4. She wrote the diary and died.
FAWN	5. 'Straight' girl Alice becomes friends with
PEANUTS	6. They were covered in acid, sending Alice on a bad trip ending with her going to the hospital.
BABBIE	7. Girl in mental hospital whose parents decide to give her up to foster care
MARCIE	8. Girl who lies to the judge and gets Alice sent to a mental hospital
BOUTIQUE	9. Kind of store Alice and Chris open
ALEX	10. Alice's younger sister
TIM	11. Alice's younger brother
CHRISTMAS	12. Alice's favorite holiday
CHRIS	13. Girl Alice runs away with
DIARY	14. What Alice locks in a metal box
HAPPINESS	15. Kitten belonging to Alice's sister; makes Alice appreciate the pleasures of life without drugs
DINNER	16. Alice makes this for her mother as a surprise for her birthday.
ROGER	17. Boy Alice really likes; he stands her up at the start of the book
JEWELRY	18. While in San Francisco, Alice works at a shop that sells this.
JAN	19. Girl who shows up high while Alice is babysitting
CHICAGO	20. City where Joel lives

Go Ask Alice Matching 1

___ 1. BOUTIQUE   A. He has a heart attack and dies.
___ 2. JOEL   B. Alice's younger sister
___ 3. BABBIE   C. Kind of store Alice and Chris open
___ 4. GRANDPA   D. Alice makes this for her mother as a surprise for her birthday.
___ 5. LARSEN   E. Kids at school threaten to hide drugs in Alice's father's ___ to get him in trouble.
___ 6. ALICE   F. Girl's house where Alice played 'Button, Button, Who's Got the Button?'
___ 7. DINNER   G. City where Joel lives
___ 8. HAPPINESS   H. Girl in mental hospital whose parents decide to give her up to foster care
___ 9. PREGNANT   I. The job of Alice's father
___ 10. DIARY   J. She wrote the diary and died.
___ 11. SHELIA   K. Chris's employer; turns the girls onto drugs in San Francisco
___ 12. JEWELRY   L. Kitten belonging to Alice's sister; makes Alice appreciate the pleasures of life without drugs
___ 13. CAR   M. Girl Alice runs away with
___ 14. JAN   N. What Alice locks in a metal box
___ 15. JILL   O. City Alice first goes to the second time she runs away
___ 16. MARCIE   P. 'Straight' girl Alice becomes friends with
___ 17. DENVER   Q. They were covered in acid, sending Alice on a bad trip ending with her going to the hospital.
___ 18. CHRIS   R. Girl who shows up high while Alice is babysitting
___ 19. FAWN   S. Girl who lies to the judge and gets Alice sent to a mental hospital
___ 20. TIM   T. Boy Alice meets at the university library; he is supportive
___ 21. ROGER   U. While in San Francisco, Alice works at a shop that sells this.
___ 22. ALEX   V. Because Alice is worried she is ___, she can't sleep, and the doctor prescribes tranquilizers.
___ 23. CHICAGO   W. Alice's younger brother
___ 24. PROFESSOR   X. Boy Alice really likes; he stands her up at the start of the book
___ 25. PEANUTS   Y. Last name of the family Alice babysits for

Go Ask Alice Matching 1 Answer Key

C - 1. BOUTIQUE	A.	He has a heart attack and dies.
T - 2. JOEL	B.	Alice's younger sister
H - 3. BABBIE	C.	Kind of store Alice and Chris open
A - 4. GRANDPA	D.	Alice makes this for her mother as a surprise for her birthday.
Y - 5. LARSEN	E.	Kids at school threaten to hide drugs in Alice's father's ___ to get him in trouble.
J - 6. ALICE	F.	Girl's house where Alice played 'Button, Button, Who's Got the Button?'
D - 7. DINNER	G.	City where Joel lives
L - 8. HAPPINESS	H.	Girl in mental hospital whose parents decide to give her up to foster care
V - 9. PREGNANT	I.	The job of Alice's father
N -10. DIARY	J.	She wrote the diary and died.
K -11. SHELIA	K.	Chris's employer; turns the girls onto drugs in San Francisco
U -12. JEWELRY	L.	Kitten belonging to Alice's sister; makes Alice appreciate the pleasures of life without drugs
E -13. CAR	M.	Girl Alice runs away with
R -14. JAN	N.	What Alice locks in a metal box
F -15. JILL	O.	City Alice first goes to the second time she runs away
S -16. MARCIE	P.	'Straight' girl Alice becomes friends with
O -17. DENVER	Q.	They were covered in acid, sending Alice on a bad trip ending with her going to the hospital.
M -18. CHRIS	R.	Girl who shows up high while Alice is babysitting
P -19. FAWN	S.	Girl who lies to the judge and gets Alice sent to a mental hospital
W -20. TIM	T.	Boy Alice meets at the university library; he is supportive
X -21. ROGER	U.	While in San Francisco, Alice works at a shop that sells this.
B -22. ALEX	V.	Because Alice is worried she is ___, she can't sleep, and the doctor prescribes tranquilizers.
G -23. CHICAGO	W.	Alice's younger brother
I - 24. PROFESSOR	X.	Boy Alice really likes; he stands her up at the start of the book
Q -25. PEANUTS	Y.	Last name of the family Alice babysits for

Go Ask Alice Matching 2

___ 1. MARCIE A. Alice's favorite holiday

___ 2. SHELIA B. While in San Francisco, Alice works at a shop that sells this.

___ 3. CHRISTMAS C. Because Alice is worried she is ___, she can't sleep, and the doctor prescribes tranquilizers.

___ 4. LETTER D. People who take Alice to the doctor & give her food & clothes

___ 5. ALICE E. She wrote the diary and died.

___ 6. PEANUTS F. The job of Alice's father

___ 7. CHRIS G. They were covered in acid, sending Alice on a bad trip ending with her going to the hospital.

___ 8. DIARY H. Chris's employer; turns the girls onto drugs in San Francisco

___ 9. CANDY I. Place Alice's parents take Chris and Alice for a fun weekend away from the kids at school

___ 10. ALEX J. Joel sends Alice this while she is in the hospital.

___ 11. CAR K. Girl who shows up high while Alice is babysitting

___ 12. GRANDMA L. Name of boyfriend who got Alice into selling drugs

___ 13. RICHIE M. Girl Alice runs away with

___ 14. MOUNTAINS N. What Alice locks in a metal box

___ 15. PROFESSOR O. Girl who lies to the judge and gets Alice sent to a mental hospital

___ 16. GRANDPA P. Girl in mental hospital whose parents decide to give her up to foster care

___ 17. FAWN Q. He has a heart attack and dies.

___ 18. JILL R. Alice stays to help her around the house over the summer.

___ 19. JEWELRY S. Alice's younger sister

___ 20. JAN T. 'Straight' girl Alice becomes friends with

___ 21. BABBIE U. Girl's house where Alice played 'Button, Button, Who's Got the Button?'

___ 22. PIANO V. Instrument Alice plays

___ 23. MISSION W. What Alice wants to put drugs on to get her younger brother to experience being high

___ 24. DINNER X. Alice makes this for her mother as a surprise for her birthday.

___ 25. PREGNANT Y. Kids at school threaten to hide drugs in Alice's father's ___ to get him in trouble.

Go Ask Alice Matching 2 Answer Key

O - 1. MARCIE	A. Alice's favorite holiday
H - 2. SHELIA	B. While in San Francisco, Alice works at a shop that sells this.
A - 3. CHRISTMAS	C. Because Alice is worried she is ___, she can't sleep, and the doctor prescribes tranquilizers.
J - 4. LETTER	D. People who take Alice to the doctor & give her food & clothes
E - 5. ALICE	E. She wrote the diary and died.
G - 6. PEANUTS	F. The job of Alice's father
M - 7. CHRIS	G. They were covered in acid, sending Alice on a bad trip ending with her going to the hospital.
N - 8. DIARY	H. Chris's employer; turns the girls onto drugs in San Francisco
W - 9. CANDY	I. Place Alice's parents take Chris and Alice for a fun weekend away from the kids at school
S - 10. ALEX	J. Joel sends Alice this while she is in the hospital.
Y - 11. CAR	K. Girl who shows up high while Alice is babysitting
R - 12. GRANDMA	L. Name of boyfriend who got Alice into selling drugs
L - 13. RICHIE	M. Girl Alice runs away with
I - 14. MOUNTAINS	N. What Alice locks in a metal box
F - 15. PROFESSOR	O. Girl who lies to the judge and gets Alice sent to a mental hospital
Q - 16. GRANDPA	P. Girl in mental hospital whose parents decide to give her up to foster care
T - 17. FAWN	Q. He has a heart attack and dies.
U - 18. JILL	R. Alice stays to help her around the house over the summer.
B - 19. JEWELRY	S. Alice's younger sister
K - 20. JAN	T. 'Straight' girl Alice becomes friends with
P - 21. BABBIE	U. Girl's house where Alice played 'Button, Button, Who's Got the Button?'
V - 22. PIANO	V. Instrument Alice plays
D - 23. MISSION	W. What Alice wants to put drugs on to get her younger brother to experience being high
X - 24. DINNER	X. Alice makes this for her mother as a surprise for her birthday.
C - 25. PREGNANT	Y. Kids at school threaten to hide drugs in Alice's father's ___ to get him in trouble.

Go Ask Alice Matching 3

___ 1. ELEMENTARY   A. Because Alice is worried she is ___, she can't sleep, and the doctor prescribes tranquilizers.
___ 2. LSD   B. Alice has fun doing this with her family after a New Year's Eve party.
___ 3. LARSEN   C. Alice is ashamed that she sells drugs at the ___ school.
___ 4. BABBIE   D. Kitten belonging to Alice's sister; makes Alice appreciate the pleasures of life without drugs
___ 5. JOEL   E. Alice's favorite holiday
___ 6. CANDY   F. City Alice first goes to the second time she runs away
___ 7. RICHIE   G. Girl Alice runs away with
___ 8. PEANUTS   H. Girl in mental hospital whose parents decide to give her up to foster care
___ 9. MARCIE   I. Alice's younger brother
___ 10. HAPPINESS   J. Last name of the family Alice babysits for
___ 11. JILL   K. Alice's younger sister
___ 12. PROFESSOR   L. Drug in Alice's Coke when she first took drugs
___ 13. CHICAGO   M. Name of boyfriend who got Alice into selling drugs
___ 14. DENVER   N. They were covered in acid, sending Alice on a bad trip ending with her going to the hospital.
___ 15. TIM   O. Boy Alice meets at the university library; he is supportive
___ 16. ALEX   P. Girl who lies to the judge and gets Alice sent to a mental hospital
___ 17. CHRISTMAS   Q. Girl who shows up high while Alice is babysitting
___ 18. CLEANING   R. Alice stays to help her around the house over the summer.
___ 19. GRANDMA   S. City where Joel lives
___ 20. JAN   T. Joel sends Alice this while she is in the hospital.
___ 21. PREGNANT   U. Girl's house where Alice played 'Button, Button, Who's Got the Button?'
___ 22. CHRIS   V. The job of Alice's father
___ 23. BOUTIQUE   W. What Alice wants to put drugs on to get her younger brother to experience being high
___ 24. JEWELRY   X. While in San Francisco, Alice works at a shop that sells this.
___ 25. LETTER   Y. Kind of store Alice and Chris open

Go Ask Alice Matching 3 Answer Key

C - 1. ELEMENTARY	A. Because Alice is worried she is ___, she can't sleep, and the doctor prescribes tranquilizers.
L - 2. LSD	B. Alice has fun doing this with her family after a New Year's Eve party.
J - 3. LARSEN	C. Alice is ashamed that she sells drugs at the ___ school.
H - 4. BABBIE	D. Kitten belonging to Alice's sister; makes Alice appreciate the pleasures of life without drugs
O - 5. JOEL	E. Alice's favorite holiday
W - 6. CANDY	F. City Alice first goes to the second time she runs away
M - 7. RICHIE	G. Girl Alice runs away with
N - 8. PEANUTS	H. Girl in mental hospital whose parents decide to give her up to foster care
P - 9. MARCIE	I. Alice's younger brother
D - 10. HAPPINESS	J. Last name of the family Alice babysits for
U - 11. JILL	K. Alice's younger sister
V - 12. PROFESSOR	L. Drug in Alice's Coke when she first took drugs
S - 13. CHICAGO	M. Name of boyfriend who got Alice into selling drugs
F - 14. DENVER	N. They were covered in acid, sending Alice on a bad trip ending with her going to the hospital.
I - 15. TIM	O. Boy Alice meets at the university library; he is supportive
K - 16. ALEX	P. Girl who lies to the judge and gets Alice sent to a mental hospital
E - 17. CHRISTMAS	Q. Girl who shows up high while Alice is babysitting
B - 18. CLEANING	R. Alice stays to help her around the house over the summer.
R - 19. GRANDMA	S. City where Joel lives
Q - 20. JAN	T. Joel sends Alice this while she is in the hospital.
A - 21. PREGNANT	U. Girl's house where Alice played 'Button, Button, Who's Got the Button?'
G - 22. CHRIS	V. The job of Alice's father
Y - 23. BOUTIQUE	W. What Alice wants to put drugs on to get her younger brother to experience being high
X - 24. JEWELRY	X. While in San Francisco, Alice works at a shop that sells this.
T - 25. LETTER	Y. Kind of store Alice and Chris open

Go Ask Alice Matching 4

___ 1. DIARY   A. The job of Alice's father
___ 2. MOUNTAINS   B. Kind of store Alice and Chris open
___ 3. LARSEN   C. Girl in mental hospital whose parents decide to give her up to foster care
___ 4. FAWN   D. Girl Alice runs away with
___ 5. HAPPINESS   E. City where Joel lives
___ 6. RICHIE   F. People who take Alice to the doctor & give her food & clothes
___ 7. CAR   G. Kitten belonging to Alice's sister; makes Alice appreciate the pleasures of life without drugs
___ 8. PROFESSOR   H. Alice's favorite holiday
___ 9. ROGER   I. 'Straight' girl Alice becomes friends with
___10. ALEX   J. They were covered in acid, sending Alice on a bad trip ending with her going to the hospital.
___11. SHELIA   K. Kids at school threaten to hide drugs in Alice's father's ___ to get him in trouble.
___12. BABBIE   L. Alice's younger sister
___13. LSD   M. She wrote the diary and died.
___14. PIANO   N. Boy Alice really likes; he stands her up at the start of the book
___15. MISSION   O. Girl who lies to the judge and gets Alice sent to a mental hospital
___16. CHRIS   P. Drug in Alice's Coke when she first took drugs
___17. BOUTIQUE   Q. He has a heart attack and dies.
___18. CHRISTMAS   R. Chris's employer; turns the girls onto drugs in San Francisco
___19. CHICAGO   S. Last name of the family Alice babysits for
___20. MARCIE   T. Place Alice's parents take Chris and Alice for a fun weekend away from the kids at school
___21. ALICE   U. Alice is ashamed that she sells drugs at the ___ school.
___22. ELEMENTARY   V. Instrument Alice plays
___23. GRANDPA   W. Boy Alice meets at the university library; he is supportive
___24. JOEL   X. Name of boyfriend who got Alice into selling drugs
___25. PEANUTS   Y. What Alice locks in a metal box

Go Ask Alice Matching 4 Answer Key

Y - 1. DIARY	A.	The job of Alice's father
T - 2. MOUNTAINS	B.	Kind of store Alice and Chris open
S - 3. LARSEN	C.	Girl in mental hospital whose parents decide to give her up to foster care
I - 4. FAWN	D.	Girl Alice runs away with
G - 5. HAPPINESS	E.	City where Joel lives
X - 6. RICHIE	F.	People who take Alice to the doctor & give her food & clothes
K - 7. CAR	G.	Kitten belonging to Alice's sister; makes Alice appreciate the pleasures of life without drugs
A - 8. PROFESSOR	H.	Alice's favorite holiday
N - 9. ROGER	I.	'Straight' girl Alice becomes friends with
L - 10. ALEX	J.	They were covered in acid, sending Alice on a bad trip ending with her going to the hospital.
R - 11. SHELIA	K.	Kids at school threaten to hide drugs in Alice's father's ___ to get him in trouble.
C - 12. BABBIE	L.	Alice's younger sister
P - 13. LSD	M.	She wrote the diary and died.
V - 14. PIANO	N.	Boy Alice really likes; he stands her up at the start of the book
F - 15. MISSION	O.	Girl who lies to the judge and gets Alice sent to a mental hospital
D - 16. CHRIS	P.	Drug in Alice's Coke when she first took drugs
B - 17. BOUTIQUE	Q.	He has a heart attack and dies.
H - 18. CHRISTMAS	R.	Chris's employer; turns the girls onto drugs in San Francisco
E - 19. CHICAGO	S.	Last name of the family Alice babysits for
O - 20. MARCIE	T.	Place Alice's parents take Chris and Alice for a fun weekend away from the kids at school
M - 21. ALICE	U.	Alice is ashamed that she sells drugs at the ___ school.
U - 22. ELEMENTARY	V.	Instrument Alice plays
Q - 23. GRANDPA	W.	Boy Alice meets at the university library; he is supportive
W - 24. JOEL	X.	Name of boyfriend who got Alice into selling drugs
J - 25. PEANUTS	Y.	What Alice locks in a metal box

Go Ask Alice Magic Squares 1

A. LARSEN E. DIARY   I. PROFESSOR M. JEWELRY
B. LETTER F. ELEMENTARY J. DENVER   N. MOUNTAINS
C. JILL   G. CHICAGO   K. BOUTIQUE   O. CHRIS
D. PIANO   H. ALEX   L. ALICE   P. CAR

1. Girl Alice runs away with
2. City Alice first goes to the second time she runs away
3. Alice's younger sister
4. Last name of the family Alice babysits for
5. Instrument Alice plays
6. What Alice locks in a metal box
7. Kind of store Alice and Chris open
8. Place Alice's parents take Chris and Alice for a fun weekend away from the kids at school
9. Alice is ashamed that she sells drugs at the ___ school.
10. Girl's house where Alice played 'Button, Button, Who's Got the Button?'
11. While in San Francisco, Alice works at a shop that sells this.
12. She wrote the diary and died.
13. The job of Alice's father
14. Kids at school threaten to hide drugs in Alice's father's ___ to get him in trouble.
15. Joel sends Alice this while she is in the hospital.
16. City where Joel lives

A=	B=	C=	D=
E=	F=	G=	H=
I=	J=	K=	L=
M=	N=	O=	P=

Go Ask Alice Magic Squares 1 Answer Key

A. LARSEN   E. DIARY   I. PROFESSOR   M. JEWELRY
B. LETTER   F. ELEMENTARY   J. DENVER   N. MOUNTAINS
C. JILL   G. CHICAGO   K. BOUTIQUE   O. CHRIS
D. PIANO   H. ALEX   L. ALICE   P. CAR

1. Girl Alice runs away with
2. City Alice first goes to the second time she runs away
3. Alice's younger sister
4. Last name of the family Alice babysits for
5. Instrument Alice plays
6. What Alice locks in a metal box
7. Kind of store Alice and Chris open
8. Place Alice's parents take Chris and Alice for a fun weekend away from the kids at school
9. Alice is ashamed that she sells drugs at the ___ school.
10. Girl's house where Alice played 'Button, Button, Who's Got the Button?'
11. While in San Francisco, Alice works at a shop that sells this.
12. She wrote the diary and died.
13. The job of Alice's father
14. Kids at school threaten to hide drugs in Alice's father's ___ to get him in trouble.
15. Joel sends Alice this while she is in the hospital.
16. City where Joel lives

A=4	B=15	C=10	D=5
E=6	F=9	G=16	H=3
I=13	J=2	K=7	L=12
M=11	N=8	O=1	P=14

Go Ask Alice Magic Squares 2

A. DINNER
B. ALEX
C. JOEL
D. PROFESSOR
E. RICHIE
F. SHELIA
G. FAWN
H. JEWELRY
I. MOUNTAINS
J. MARCIE
K. PIANO
L. CAR
M. JAN
N. LETTER
O. JILL
P. CHRIS

1. Boy Alice meets at the university library; he is supportive
2. Girl who lies to the judge and gets Alice sent to a mental hospital
3. Chris's employer; turns the girls onto drugs in San Francisco
4. Girl's house where Alice played 'Button, Button, Who's Got the Button?'
5. Girl Alice runs away with
6. Name of boyfriend who got Alice into selling drugs
7. Place Alice's parents take Chris and Alice for a fun weekend away from the kids at school
8. The job of Alice's father
9. Girl who shows up high while Alice is babysitting
10. While in San Francisco, Alice works at a shop that sells this.
11. Kids at school threaten to hide drugs in Alice's father's ___ to get him in trouble.
12. Alice makes this for her mother as a surprise for her birthday.
13. Alice's younger sister
14. Instrument Alice plays
15. 'Straight' girl Alice becomes friends with
16. Joel sends Alice this while she is in the hospital.

A=	B=	C=	D=
E=	F=	G=	H=
I=	J=	K=	L=
M=	N=	O=	P=

Go Ask Alice Magic Squares 2 Answer Key

A. DINNER
B. ALEX
C. JOEL
D. PROFESSOR
E. RICHIE
F. SHELIA
G. FAWN
H. JEWELRY
I. MOUNTAINS
J. MARCIE
K. PIANO
L. CAR
M. JAN
N. LETTER
O. JILL
P. CHRIS

1. Boy Alice meets at the university library; he is supportive
2. Girl who lies to the judge and gets Alice sent to a mental hospital
3. Chris's employer; turns the girls onto drugs in San Francisco
4. Girl's house where Alice played 'Button, Button, Who's Got the Button?'
5. Girl Alice runs away with
6. Name of boyfriend who got Alice into selling drugs
7. Place Alice's parents take Chris and Alice for a fun weekend away from the kids at school
8. The job of Alice's father
9. Girl who shows up high while Alice is babysitting
10. While in San Francisco, Alice works at a shop that sells this.
11. Kids at school threaten to hide drugs in Alice's father's ___ to get him in trouble.
12. Alice makes this for her mother as a surprise for her birthday.
13. Alice's younger sister
14. Instrument Alice plays
15. 'Straight' girl Alice becomes friends with
16. Joel sends Alice this while she is in the hospital.

A=12	B=13	C=1	D=8
E=6	F=3	G=15	H=10
I=7	J=2	K=14	L=11
M=9	N=16	O=4	P=5

Go Ask Alice Magic Squares 3

A. ALICE
B. JOEL
C. FAWN
D. LSD
E. CAR
F. JILL
G. TIM
H. PIANO
I. CHRISTMAS
J. MOUNTAINS
K. ELEMENTARY
L. CHICAGO
M. MISSION
N. GRANDMA
O. CANDY
P. JAN

1. People who take Alice to the doctor & give her food & clothes
2. Girl's house where Alice played 'Button, Button, Who's Got the Button?'
3. Instrument Alice plays
4. What Alice wants to put drugs on to get her younger brother to experience being high
5. City where Joel lives
6. 'Straight' girl Alice becomes friends with
7. She wrote the diary and died.
8. Place Alice's parents take Chris and Alice for a fun weekend away from the kids at school
9. Alice is ashamed that she sells drugs at the ___ school.
10. Drug in Alice's Coke when she first took drugs
11. Boy Alice meets at the university library; he is supportive
12. Alice's favorite holiday
13. Alice stays to help her around the house over the summer.
14. Kids at school threaten to hide drugs in Alice's father's ___ to get him in trouble.
15. Alice's younger brother
16. Girl who shows up high while Alice is babysitting

A=	B=	C=	D=
E=	F=	G=	H=
I=	J=	K=	L=
M=	N=	O=	P=

Go Ask Alice Magic Squares 3 Answer Key

A. ALICE   E. CAR   I. CHRISTMAS   M. MISSION
B. JOEL   F. JILL   J. MOUNTAINS   N. GRANDMA
C. FAWN   G. TIM   K. ELEMENTARY   O. CANDY
D. LSD   H. PIANO   L. CHICAGO   P. JAN

1. People who take Alice to the doctor & give her food & clothes
2. Girl's house where Alice played 'Button, Button, Who's Got the Button?'
3. Instrument Alice plays
4. What Alice wants to put drugs on to get her younger brother to experience being high
5. City where Joel lives
6. 'Straight' girl Alice becomes friends with
7. She wrote the diary and died.
8. Place Alice's parents take Chris and Alice for a fun weekend away from the kids at school
9. Alice is ashamed that she sells drugs at the ___ school.
10. Drug in Alice's Coke when she first took drugs
11. Boy Alice meets at the university library; he is supportive
12. Alice's favorite holiday
13. Alice stays to help her around the house over the summer.
14. Kids at school threaten to hide drugs in Alice's father's ___ to get him in trouble.
15. Alice's younger brother
16. Girl who shows up high while Alice is babysitting

A=7	B=11	C=6	D=10
E=14	F=2	G=15	H=3
I=12	J=8	K=9	L=5
M=1	N=13	O=4	P=16

Go Ask Alice Magic Squares 4

A. SHELIA
B. BABBIE
C. JILL
D. RICHIE
E. CHRIS
F. CHICAGO
G. BOUTIQUE
H. MOUNTAINS
I. PREGNANT
J. JOEL
K. DINNER
L. MISSION
M. CLEANING
N. PEANUTS
O. LARSEN
P. ALEX

1. Place Alice's parents take Chris and Alice for a fun weekend away from the kids at school
2. Alice has fun doing this with her family after a New Year's Eve party.
3. Girl in mental hospital whose parents decide to give her up to foster care
4. Alice makes this for her mother as a surprise for her birthday.
5. Boy Alice meets at the university library; he is supportive
6. Girl's house where Alice played 'Button, Button, Who's Got the Button?'
7. Alice's younger sister
8. Girl Alice runs away with
9. Last name of the family Alice babysits for
10. City where Joel lives
11. Because Alice is worried she is ___, she can't sleep, and the doctor prescribes tranquilizers.
12. Name of boyfriend who got Alice into selling drugs
13. Chris's employer; turns the girls onto drugs in San Francisco
14. People who take Alice to the doctor & give her food & clothes
15. Kind of store Alice and Chris open
16. They were covered in acid, sending Alice on a bad trip ending with her going to the hospi to the hospital.

A=	B=	C=	D=
E=	F=	G=	H=
I=	J=	K=	L=
M=	N=	O=	P=

Go Ask Alice Magic Squares 4 Answer Key

A. SHELIA
B. BABBIE
C. JILL
D. RICHIE
E. CHRIS
F. CHICAGO
G. BOUTIQUE
H. MOUNTAINS
I. PREGNANT
J. JOEL
K. DINNER
L. MISSION
M. CLEANING
N. PEANUTS
O. LARSEN
P. ALEX

1. Place Alice's parents take Chris and Alice for a fun weekend away from the kids at school
2. Alice has fun doing this with her family after a New Year's Eve party.
3. Girl in mental hospital whose parents decide to give her up to foster care
4. Alice makes this for her mother as a surprise for her birthday.
5. Boy Alice meets at the university library; he is supportive
6. Girl's house where Alice played 'Button, Button, Who's Got the Button?'
7. Alice's younger sister
8. Girl Alice runs away with
9. Last name of the family Alice babysits for
10. City where Joel lives
11. Because Alice is worried she is ___, she can't sleep, and the doctor prescribes tranquilizers.
12. Name of boyfriend who got Alice into selling drugs
13. Chris's employer; turns the girls onto drugs in San Francisco
14. People who take Alice to the doctor & give her food & clothes
15. Kind of store Alice and Chris open
16. They were covered in acid, sending Alice on a bad trip ending with her going to the hospi to the hospital.

A=13	B=3	C=6	D=12
E=8	F=10	G=15	H=1
I=11	J=5	K=4	L=14
M=2	N=16	O=9	P=7

Go Ask Alice Word Search 1

```
C H R I S T M A S H A P P I N E S S Q R
H S Z D F M N N C L E U Q I T U O B L W
I R P E R H Y D C V V M W M A G F S K R
C N F N D F F R P J S D O Q K N Y Z H P
A J J V J C D R X E M Q B U C N O V W K
G N L E B P E J R W A C A S N L Y H Y Y
O Z G R D G J H O E R S B T F T P R G Z
D K R Q N J F M G L C H B U A M A M R B
B I A A K Q R W E R I L I N W T G I A V
J A N D I A R Y R Y E S E A N D Y S N L
Q T D N C C E Y W O I S L E L D D S D S
T R M T E E T W J R R S M P N E T I P D
B I A Y I R T C H A Q E H A Q V X O A L
D N M H H D E C L A L I C E J Z M N D W
S G C D S Q L J X E C S B F L I W P X C
C I Q L C Z Z F Y B H R N Y D I L Z B J
R D G V M P R O F E S S O R C C A L R K
W Z D L M K C H Q S C L E A N I N G K C
```

'Straight' girl Alice becomes friends with (4)
Alice has fun doing this with her family after a New Year's Eve party. (8)
Alice is ashamed that she sells drugs at the ___ school. (10)
Alice makes this for her mother as a surprise for her birthday. (6)
Alice stays to help her around the house over the summer. (7)
Alice's favorite holiday (9)
Alice's younger brother (3)
Alice's younger sister (4)
Because Alice is worried she is ___, she can't sleep, and the doctor prescribes tranquilizers. (8)
Boy Alice meets at the university library; he is supportive (4)
Boy Alice really likes; he stands her up at the start of the book (5)
Chris's employer; turns the girls onto drugs in San Francisco (6)
City Alice first goes to the second time she runs away (6)
City where Joel lives (7)
Drug in Alice's Coke when she first took drugs (3)
Girl Alice runs away with (5)
Girl in mental hospital whose parents decide to give her up to foster care (6)
Girl who lies to the judge and gets Alice sent to a mental hospital (6)
Girl who shows up high while Alice is babysitting (3)
Girl's house where Alice played 'Button, Button, Who's Got the Button?' (4)
He has a heart attack and dies. (7)
Instrument Alice plays (5)
Joel sends Alice this while she is in the hospital. (6)
Kids at school threaten to hide drugs in Alice's father's ___ to get him in trouble. (3)
Kind of store Alice and Chris open (8)
Kitten belonging to Alice's sister; makes Alice appreciate the pleasures of life without drugs (9)
Last name of the family Alice babysits for (6)
Name of boyfriend who got Alice into selling drugs (6)
People who take Alice to the doctor & give her food & clothes (7)
Place Alice's parents take Chris and Alice for a fun weekend away from the kids at school (9)
She wrote the diary and died. (5)
The job of Alice's father (9)
They were covered in acid, sending Alice on a bad trip ending with her going to the hospital. (7)
What Alice locks in a metal box (5)
What Alice wants to put drugs on to get her younger brother to experience being high (5)
While in San Francisco, Alice works at a shop that sells this. (7)

Go Ask Alice Word Search 1 Answer Key

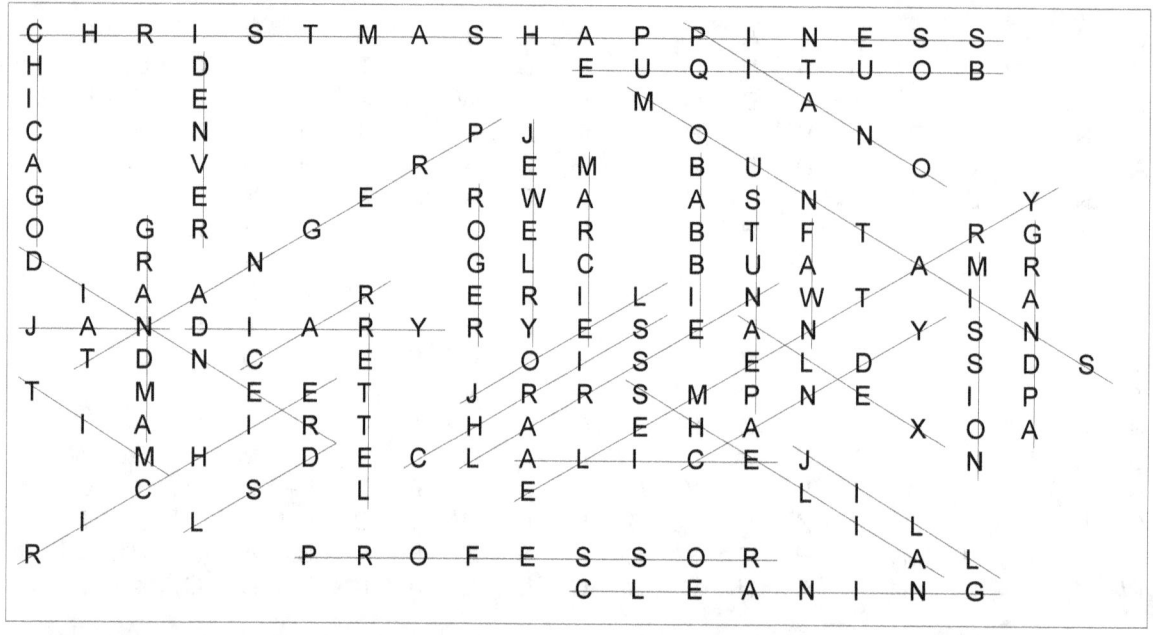

'Straight' girl Alice becomes friends with (4)
Alice has fun doing this with her family after a New Year's Eve party. (8)
Alice is ashamed that she sells drugs at the ___ school. (10)
Alice makes this for her mother as a surprise for her birthday. (6)
Alice stays to help her around the house over the summer. (7)
Alice's favorite holiday (9)
Alice's younger brother (3)
Alice's younger sister (4)
Because Alice is worried she is ___, she can't sleep, and the doctor prescribes tranquilizers. (8)
Boy Alice meets at the university library; he is supportive (4)
Boy Alice really likes; he stands her up at the start of the book (5)
Chris's employer; turns the girls onto drugs in San Francisco (6)
City Alice first goes to the second time she runs away (6)
City where Joel lives (7)
Drug in Alice's Coke when she first took drugs (3)
Girl Alice runs away with (5)
Girl in mental hospital whose parents decide to give her up to foster care (6)
Girl who lies to the judge and gets Alice sent to a mental hospital (6)
Girl who shows up high while Alice is babysitting (3)
Girl's house where Alice played 'Button, Button, Who's Got the Button?' (4)
He has a heart attack and dies. (7)
Instrument Alice plays (5)
Joel sends Alice this while she is in the hospital. (6)
Kids at school threaten to hide drugs in Alice's father's ___ to get him in trouble. (3)
Kind of store Alice and Chris open (8)
Kitten belonging to Alice's sister; makes Alice appreciate the pleasures of life without drugs (9)
Last name of the family Alice babysits for (6)
Name of boyfriend who got Alice into selling drugs (6)
People who take Alice to the doctor & give her food & clothes (7)
Place Alice's parents take Chris and Alice for a fun weekend away from the kids at school (9)
She wrote the diary and died. (5)
The job of Alice's father (9)
They were covered in acid, sending Alice on a bad trip ending with her going to the hospital. (7)
What Alice locks in a metal box (5)
What Alice wants to put drugs on to get her younger brother to experience being high (5)
While in San Francisco, Alice works at a shop that sells this. (7)

Go Ask Alice Word Search 2

```
P E A N U T S B A L I C E I H C I R X R
R T E A B Z G A W J R V F A A X H E C G
O T U P S X K B T Q S K P N F S L R H S
F P Q D L H C B M N N P D M J A D W I L
E D I N N E R I H N I Y L E T T E R C S
S B T A J L G E A N W B S I H X N D A V
S L U R N P N J E M H W D C K K V C G D
O Y O G L O Y S F G H M F R J R E H O V
R G B L A R S E N T I M A A G B R R E Q
J I L L A O Q K Y S O F W M N Y A I L X
P W M I R G C G S U J P N Q I Z C S E K
Y R D C Q E G I N B H E H P N S B T M K
X D E L N R O T F J Y N W Q A X F M E H
J D T G Q N A W H J C X D E E V J A N N
T C Q B N I P F Y P L S H E L I A S T Z
N A M D N A R G Z L R V Y E C R M Z A H
V N K S K X N Q L R S B O S G C Y K R F
G N Q G T J X T Z G B J X N X P D L Y B
```

'Straight' girl Alice becomes friends with (4)
Alice has fun doing this with her family after a New Year's Eve party. (8)
Alice is ashamed that she sells drugs at the ___ school. (10)
Alice makes this for her mother as a surprise for her birthday. (6)
Alice stays to help her around the house over the summer. (7)
Alice's favorite holiday (9)
Alice's younger brother (3)
Alice's younger sister (4)
Because Alice is worried she is ___, she can't sleep, and the doctor prescribes tranquilizers. (8)
Boy Alice meets at the university library; he is supportive (4)
Boy Alice really likes; he stands her up at the start of the book (5)
Chris's employer; turns the girls onto drugs in San Francisco (6)
City Alice first goes to the second time she runs away (6)
City where Joel lives (7)
Drug in Alice's Coke when she first took drugs (3)
Girl Alice runs away with (5)
Girl in mental hospital whose parents decide to give her up to foster care (6)
Girl who lies to the judge and gets Alice sent to a mental hospital (6)

Girl who shows up high while Alice is babysitting (3)
Girl's house where Alice played 'Button, Button, Who's Got the Button?' (4)
He has a heart attack and dies. (7)
Instrument Alice plays (5)
Joel sends Alice this while she is in the hospital. (6)
Kids at school threaten to hide drugs in Alice's father's ___ to get him in trouble. (3)
Kind of store Alice and Chris open (8)
Kitten belonging to Alice's sister; makes Alice appreciate the pleasures of life without drugs (9)
Last name of the family Alice babysits for (6)
Name of boyfriend who got Alice into selling drugs (6)
People who take Alice to the doctor & give her food & clothes (7)
Place Alice's parents take Chris and Alice for a fun weekend away from the kids at school (9)
She wrote the diary and died. (5)
The job of Alice's father (9)
They were covered in acid, sending Alice on a bad trip ending with her going to the hospital. (7)
What Alice locks in a metal box (5)
What Alice wants to put drugs on to get her younger brother to experience being high (5)
While in San Francisco, Alice works at a shop that sells this. (7)

Go Ask Alice Word Search 2 Answer Key

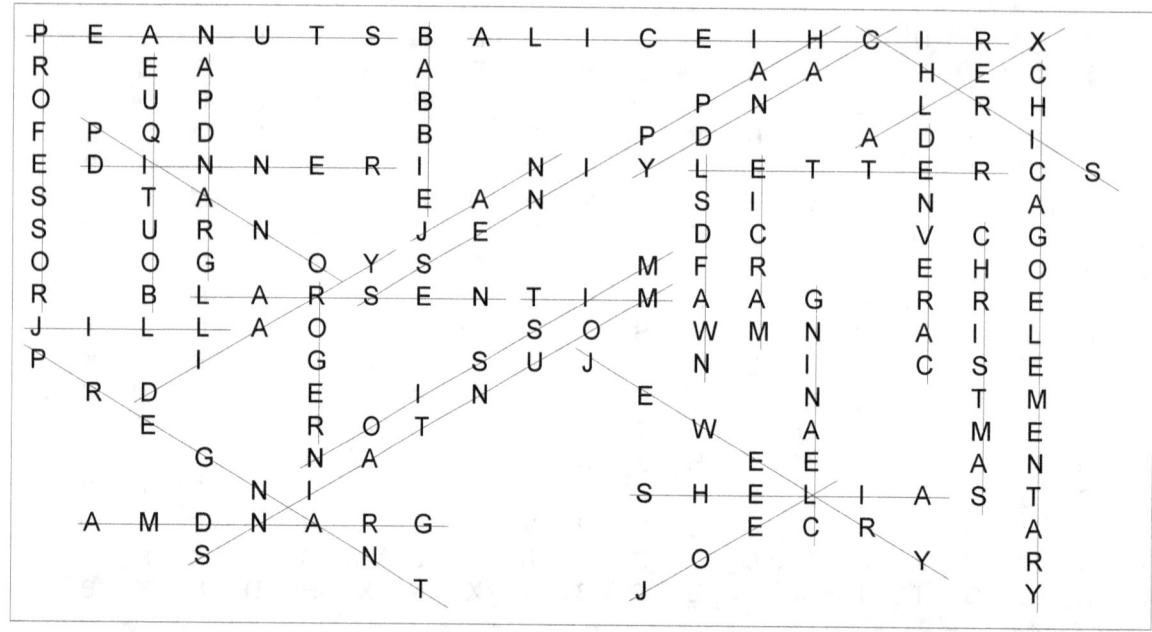

'Straight' girl Alice becomes friends with (4)
Alice has fun doing this with her family after a New Year's Eve party. (8)
Alice is ashamed that she sells drugs at the ___ school. (10)
Alice makes this for her mother as a surprise for her birthday. (6)
Alice stays to help her around the house over the summer. (7)
Alice's favorite holiday (9)
Alice's younger brother (3)
Alice's younger sister (4)
Because Alice is worried she is ___, she can't sleep, and the doctor prescribes tranquilizers. (8)
Boy Alice meets at the university library; he is supportive (4)
Boy Alice really likes; he stands her up at the start of the book (5)
Chris's employer; turns the girls onto drugs in San Francisco (6)
City Alice first goes to the second time she runs away (6)
City where Joel lives (7)
Drug in Alice's Coke when she first took drugs (3)
Girl Alice runs away with (5)
Girl in mental hospital whose parents decide to give her up to foster care (6)
Girl who lies to the judge and gets Alice sent to a mental hospital (6)

Girl who shows up high while Alice is babysitting (3)
Girl's house where Alice played 'Button, Button, Who's Got the Button?' (4)
He has a heart attack and dies. (7)
Instrument Alice plays (5)
Joel sends Alice this while she is in the hospital. (6)
Kids at school threaten to hide drugs in Alice's father's ___ to get him in trouble. (3)
Kind of store Alice and Chris open (8)
Kitten belonging to Alice's sister; makes Alice appreciate the pleasures of life without drugs (9)
Last name of the family Alice babysits for (6)
Name of boyfriend who got Alice into selling drugs (6)
People who take Alice to the doctor & give her food & clothes (7)
Place Alice's parents take Chris and Alice for a fun weekend away from the kids at school (9)
She wrote the diary and died. (5)
The job of Alice's father (9)
They were covered in acid, sending Alice on a bad trip ending with her going to the hospital. (7)
What Alice locks in a metal box (5)
What Alice wants to put drugs on to get her younger brother to experience being high (5)
While in San Francisco, Alice works at a shop that sells this. (7)

Go Ask Alice Word Search 3

```
P E A N U T S R O G E R G R A N D P A G
I E R H N V I M R L J Q P Z X N E B X H
A N L C X C R A I Z Q I B K N Q N P M W
N C P E H D N E N S H E L I A H V D C P
O M L I M D W U K Z S G C L L L E S A G
  A E T M E Z Q F F J I L Y L R R N D K
J Y X A T X N I J B M P O S X C P M D K
M A L I C E S T S N I A T N U O M N Y N
M A C Y Y P I U A W Z M Q J P D M M C X
N C R N W M R O K R C P C R S G K L L S
J H R C W R F B L N Y J E D S R B G E X
K I D D I P V L W B Q G J W E R L W A M
H C V C H E M P D N N F E D N L G M N P
Q A W D Q M F G I A N E W C I E R B I Q
Y G C B Q D Z R N F D I E R P T V C N Q
J O W L P G I T N L Y B L H P T L E G Q
N Z S M Y F W A E Z C B R Y A E S S D G
P R O F E S S O R T X A Y C H R I S D M
V Y R X Q D J B V Y J B R K A L P M R Y
C H R I S T M A S F A W N L Y J A N V Z
```

ALEX	CHRISTMAS	GRANDPA	LSD	RICHIE
ALICE	CLEANING	HAPPINESS	MARCIE	ROGER
BABBIE	DENVER	JAN	MISSION	SHELIA
BOUTIQUE	DIARY	JEWELRY	MOUNTAINS	TIM
CANDY	DINNER	JILL	PEANUTS	
CAR	ELEMENTARY	JOEL	PIANO	
CHICAGO	FAWN	LARSEN	PREGNANT	
CHRIS	GRANDMA	LETTER	PROFESSOR	

Go Ask Alice Word Search 3 Answer Key

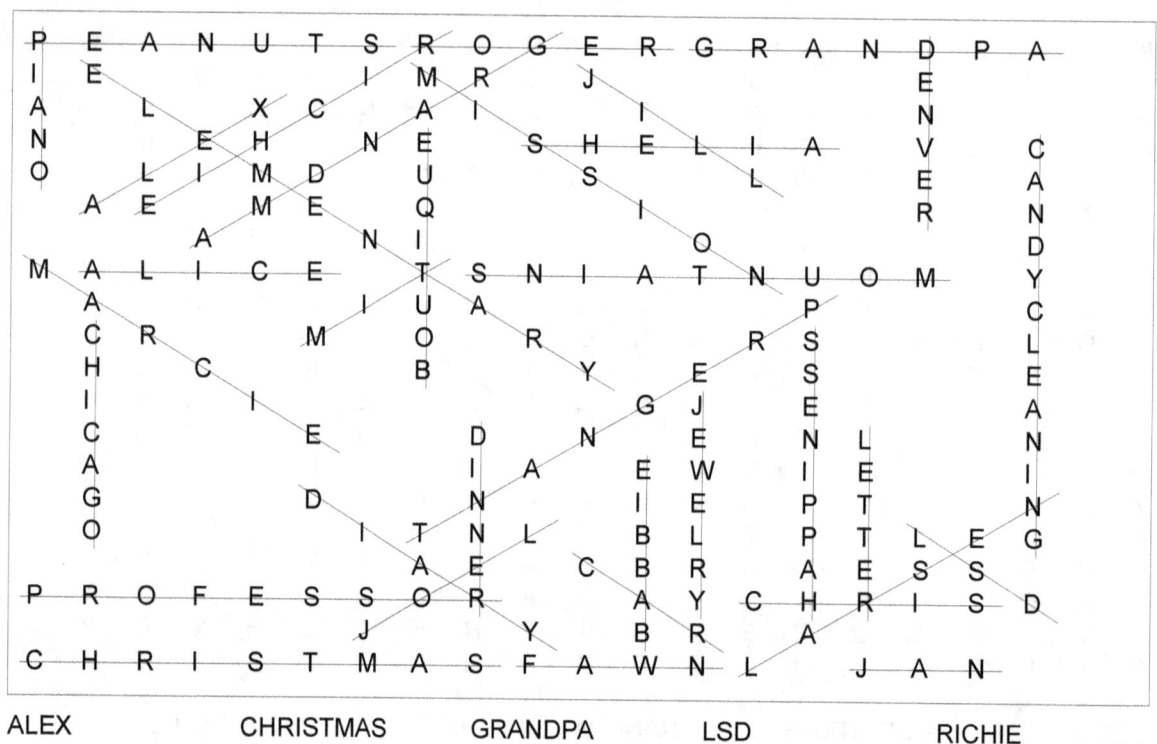

ALEX	CHRISTMAS	GRANDPA	LSD	RICHIE
ALICE	CLEANING	HAPPINESS	MARCIE	ROGER
BABBIE	DENVER	JAN	MISSION	SHELIA
BOUTIQUE	DIARY	JEWELRY	MOUNTAINS	TIM
CANDY	DINNER	JILL	PEANUTS	
CAR	ELEMENTARY	JOEL	PIANO	
CHICAGO	FAWN	LARSEN	PREGNANT	
CHRIS	GRANDMA	LETTER	PROFESSOR	

Go Ask Alice Word Search 4

```
C A N D Y B P G R A N D M A S Y R L T G
L J M V Y O E V X B L N Z A P T I E S
E H O S R U A K F S X I M M M L C T K
A D U N F T N J Z Z K T C C H H T P F
N D N O L I U K J B S N J E H J I P N
I Y T I T Q U T F W I E F M E Z R E R Z
N L A S S U S W R S L C P L W C H H Y
G N I S K E C H R G R L L Y Y R N H
G S N I H R C A W E B C R R V O L B M
P C S M D E L B G H R J A L S C F R Z W
Q X V J H Y L O V D X I Y S V X Q C Y L
M M Z J R F R I L G D R E I B B A B W W
T P S S R C R R A Q A F C V J V Z R L N
D R P Z F J Y G G T O M A H M V Z P K
Z E M H H B D H N R R P R X I P D T P E
V G G D J X R E P R D K E R B C D I V N
F N L C I O C M Q N N Z W N B G N A C M
V A H T E E A D A V L Q N V J W R G N M
C N X E L A B R S S E N I P P A H D O M
P T N E K G G Q F J R R D V M F N L S D
```

ALEX   CHRISTMAS   GRANDPA   LSD   RICHIE

ALICE   CLEANING   HAPPINESS   MARCIE   ROGER

BABBIE   DENVER   JAN   MISSION   SHELIA

BOUTIQUE   DIARY   JEWELRY   MOUNTAINS   TIM

CANDY   DINNER   JILL   PEANUTS

CAR   ELEMENTARY   JOEL   PIANO

CHICAGO   FAWN   LARSEN   PREGNANT

CHRIS   GRANDMA   LETTER   PROFESSOR

Go Ask Alice Word Search 4 Answer Key

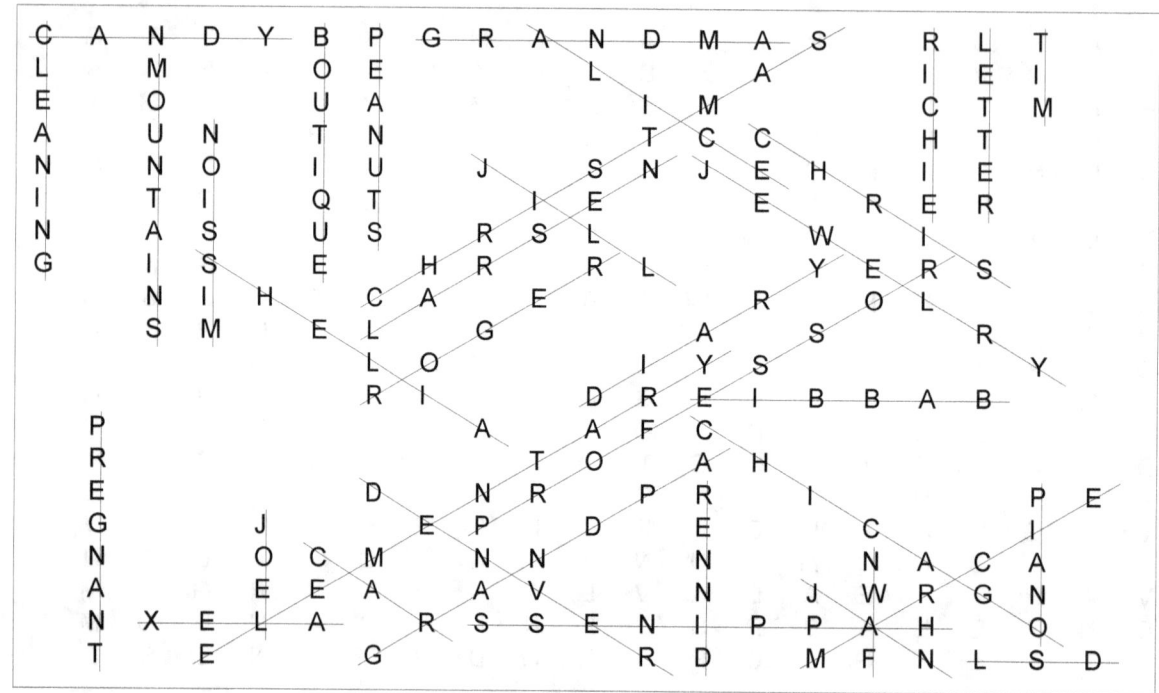

ALEX	CHRISTMAS	GRANDPA	LSD	RICHIE
ALICE	CLEANING	HAPPINESS	MARCIE	ROGER
BABBIE	DENVER	JAN	MISSION	SHELIA
BOUTIQUE	DIARY	JEWELRY	MOUNTAINS	TIM
CANDY	DINNER	JILL	PEANUTS	
CAR	ELEMENTARY	JOEL	PIANO	
CHICAGO	FAWN	LARSEN	PREGNANT	
CHRIS	GRANDMA	LETTER	PROFESSOR	

Go Ask Alice Crossword 1

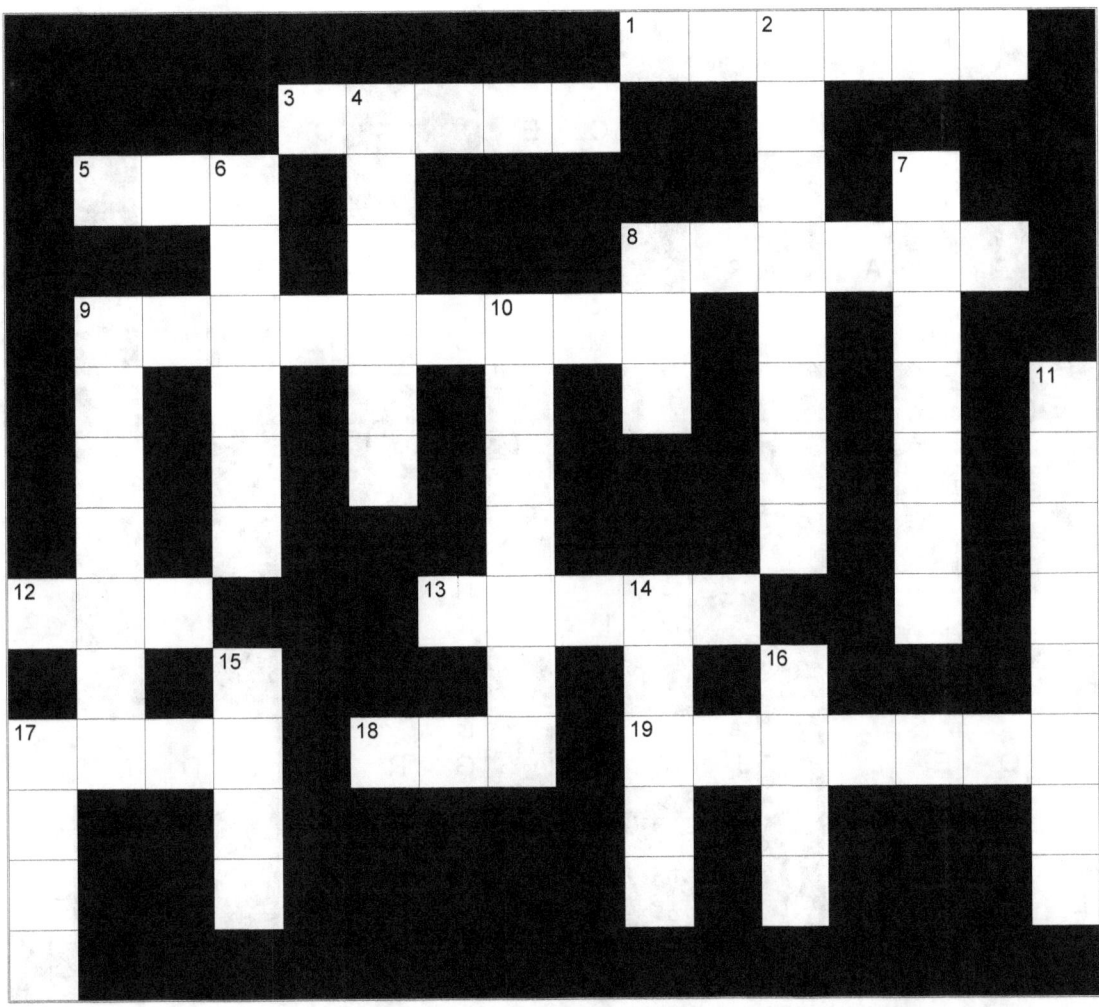

Across
1. Girl in mental hospital whose parents decide to give her up to foster care
3. She wrote the diary and died.
5. Alice's younger brother
8. Joel sends Alice this while she is in the hospital.
9. Alice's favorite holiday
12. Kids at school threaten to hide drugs in Alice's father's ___ to get him in trouble.
13. What Alice locks in a metal box
17. Boy Alice meets at the university library; he is supportive
18. Girl who shows up high while Alice is babysitting
19. Alice stays to help her around the house over the summer.

Down
2. Kind of store Alice and Chris open
4. Last name of the family Alice babysits for
6. Girl who lies to the judge and gets Alice sent to a mental hospital
7. While in San Francisco, Alice works at a shop that sells this.
8. Drug in Alice's Coke when she first took drugs
9. City where Joel lives
10. People who take Alice to the doctor & give her food & clothes
11. Because Alice is worried she is ___, she can't sleep, and the doctor prescribes tranquilizers.
14. Boy Alice really likes; he stands her up at the start of the book
15. Alice's younger sister
16. 'Straight' girl Alice becomes friends with
17. Girl's house where Alice played 'Button, Button, Who's Got the Button?'

Go Ask Alice Crossword 1 Answer Key

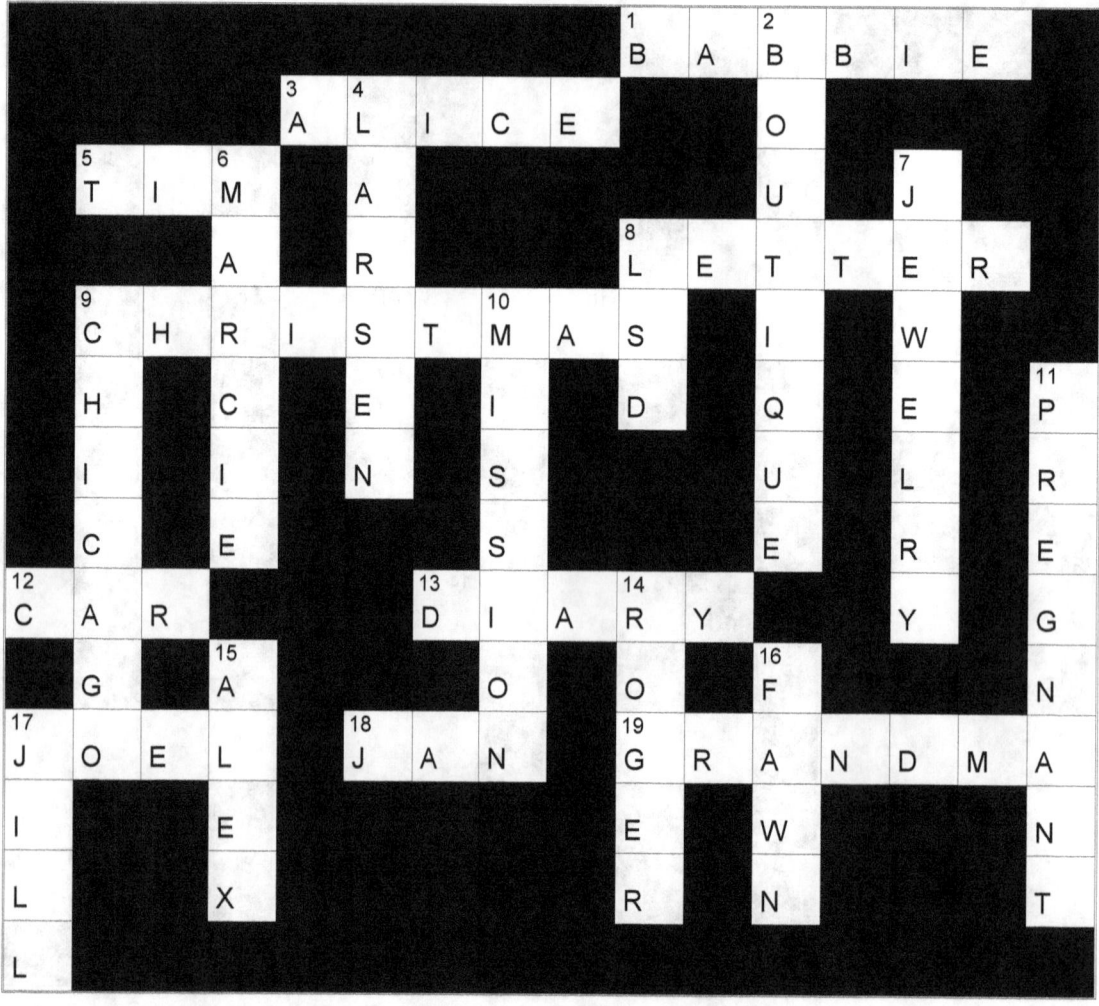

Across
1. Girl in mental hospital whose parents decide to give her up to foster care
3. She wrote the diary and died.
5. Alice's younger brother
8. Joel sends Alice this while she is in the hospital.
9. Alice's favorite holiday
12. Kids at school threaten to hide drugs in Alice's father's ___ to get him in trouble.
13. What Alice locks in a metal box
17. Boy Alice meets at the university library; he is supportive
18. Girl who shows up high while Alice is babysitting
19. Alice stays to help her around the house over the summer.

Down
2. Kind of store Alice and Chris open
4. Last name of the family Alice babysits for
6. Girl who lies to the judge and gets Alice sent to a mental hospital
7. While in San Francisco, Alice works at a shop that sells this.
8. Drug in Alice's Coke when she first took drugs
9. City where Joel lives
10. People who take Alice to the doctor & give her food & clothes
11. Because Alice is worried she is ___, she can't sleep, and the doctor prescribes tranquilizers.
14. Boy Alice really likes; he stands her up at the start of the book
15. Alice's younger sister
16. 'Straight' girl Alice becomes friends with
17. Girl's house where Alice played 'Button, Button, Who's Got the Button?'

Go Ask Alice Crossword 2

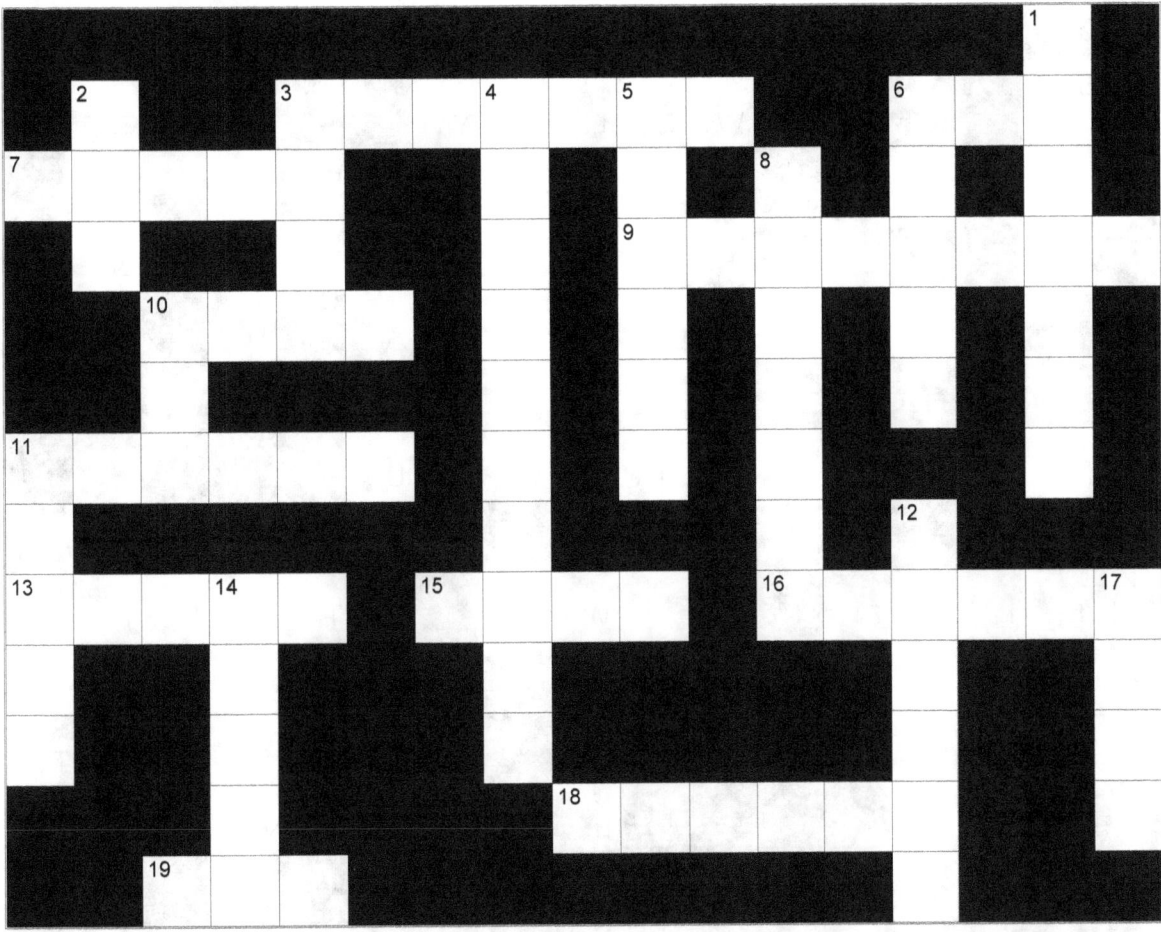

Across
3. While in San Francisco, Alice works at a shop that sells this.
6. Kids at school threaten to hide drugs in Alice's father's ___ to get him in trouble.
7. Instrument Alice plays
9. Alice has fun doing this with her family after a New Year's Eve party.
10. Girl's house where Alice played 'Button, Button, Who's Got the Button?'
11. Alice makes this for her mother as a surprise for her birthday.
13. She wrote the diary and died.
15. 'Straight' girl Alice becomes friends with
16. Chris's employer; turns the girls onto drugs in San Francisco
18. Girl in mental hospital whose parents decide to give her up to foster care
19. Drug in Alice's Coke when she first took drugs

Down
1. He has a heart attack and dies.
2. Alice's younger brother
3. Boy Alice meets at the university library; he is supportive
4. Alice is ashamed that she sells drugs at the ___ school.
5. Name of boyfriend who got Alice into selling drugs
6. What Alice wants to put drugs on to get her younger brother to experience being high
8. They were covered in acid, sending Alice on a bad trip ending with her going to the hospital.
10. Girl who shows up high while Alice is babysitting
11. What Alice locks in a metal box
12. Joel sends Alice this while she is in the hospital.
14. Girl Alice runs away with
17. Alice's younger sister

Go Ask Alice Crossword 2 Answer Key

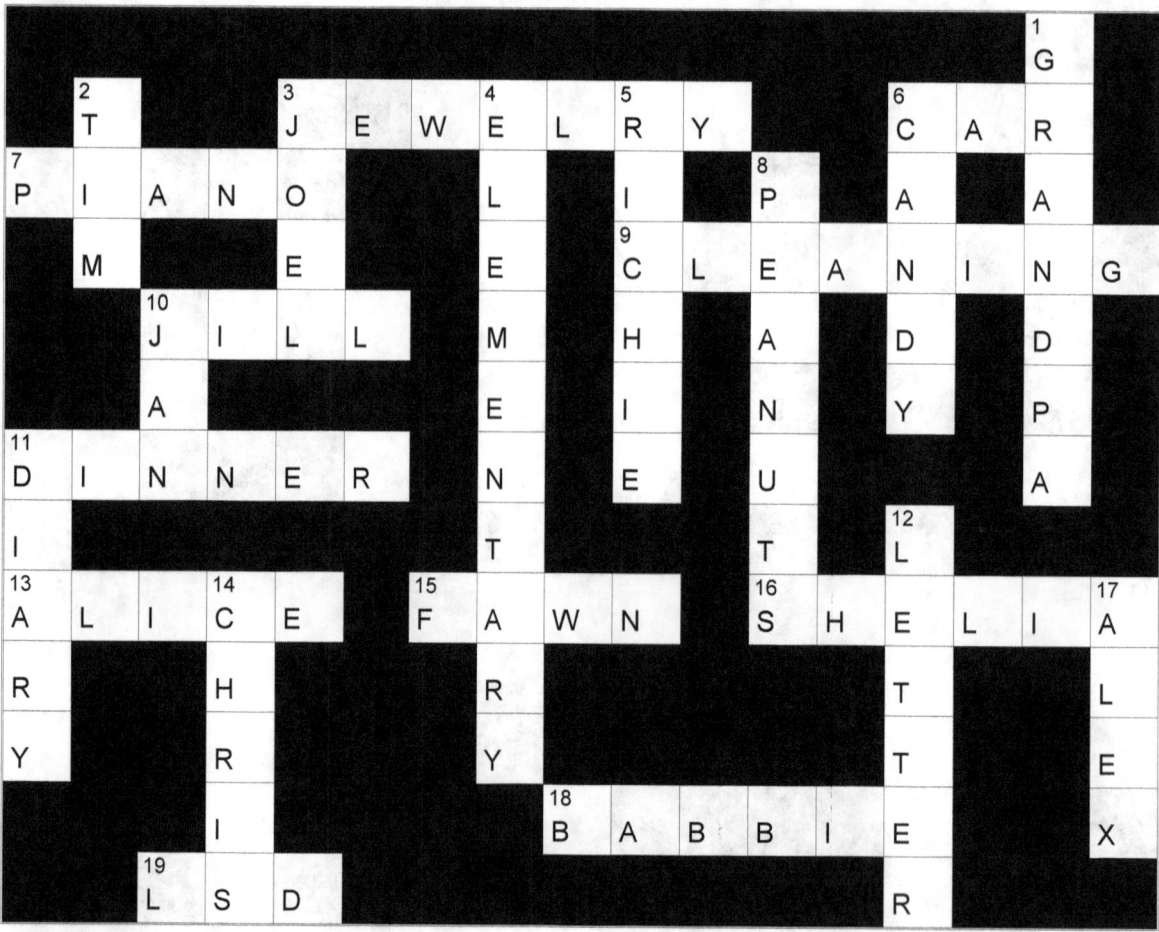

Across

3. While in San Francisco, Alice works at a shop that sells this.
6. Kids at school threaten to hide drugs in Alice's father's ___ to get him in trouble.
7. Instrument Alice plays
9. Alice has fun doing this with her family after a New Year's Eve party.
10. Girl's house where Alice played 'Button, Button, Who's Got the Button?'
11. Alice makes this for her mother as a surprise for her birthday.
13. She wrote the diary and died.
15. 'Straight' girl Alice becomes friends with
16. Chris's employer; turns the girls onto drugs in San Francisco
18. Girl in mental hospital whose parents decide to give her up to foster care
19. Drug in Alice's Coke when she first took drugs

Down

1. He has a heart attack and dies.
2. Alice's younger brother
3. Boy Alice meets at the university library; he is supportive
4. Alice is ashamed that she sells drugs at the ___ school.
5. Name of boyfriend who got Alice into selling drugs
6. What Alice wants to put drugs on to get her younger brother to experience being high
8. They were covered in acid, sending Alice on a bad trip ending with her going to the hospital.
10. Girl who shows up high while Alice is babysitting
11. What Alice locks in a metal box
12. Joel sends Alice this while she is in the hospital.
14. Girl Alice runs away with
17. Alice's younger sister

Go Ask Alice Crossword 3

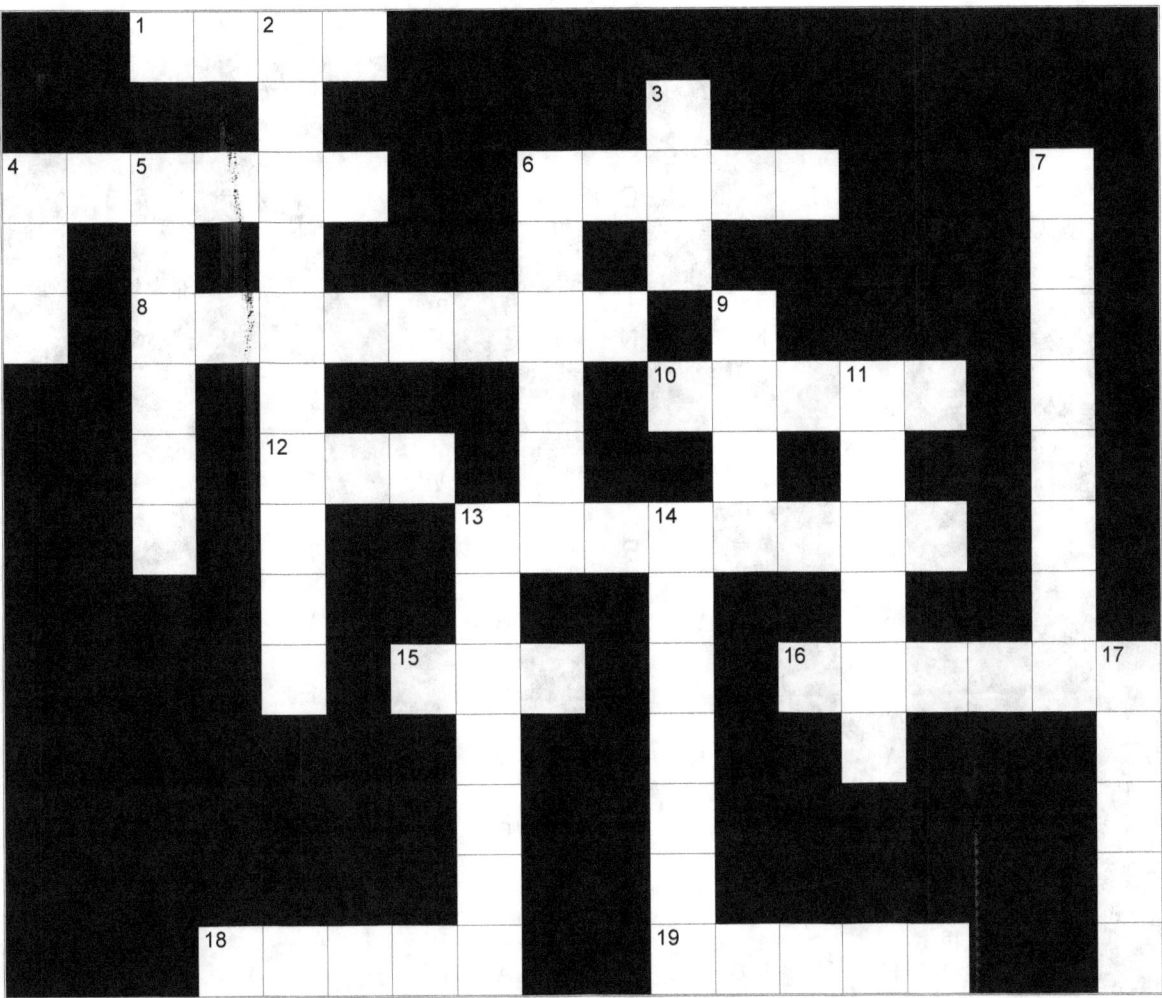

Across

1. Alice's younger sister
4. Last name of the family Alice babysits for
6. What Alice locks in a metal box
8. Alice has fun doing this with her family after a New Year's Eve party.
10. What Alice wants to put drugs on to get her younger brother to experience being high
12. Alice's younger brother
13. Because Alice is worried she is ___, she can't sleep, and the doctor prescribes tranquilizers.
15. Kids at school threaten to hide drugs in Alice's father's ___ to get him in trouble.
16. Joel sends Alice this while she is in the hospital.
18. Girl Alice runs away with
19. She wrote the diary and died.

Down

2. Alice is ashamed that she sells drugs at the ___ school.
3. Girl who shows up high while Alice is babysitting
4. Drug in Alice's Coke when she first took drugs
5. Name of boyfriend who got Alice into selling drugs
6. Alice makes this for her mother as a surprise for her birthday.
7. Kind of store Alice and Chris open
9. 'Straight' girl Alice becomes friends with
11. City Alice first goes to the second time she runs away
13. They were covered in acid, sending Alice on a bad trip ending with her going to the hospital.
14. He has a heart attack and dies.
17. Boy Alice really likes; he stands her up at the start of the book

Go Ask Alice Crossword 3 Answer Key

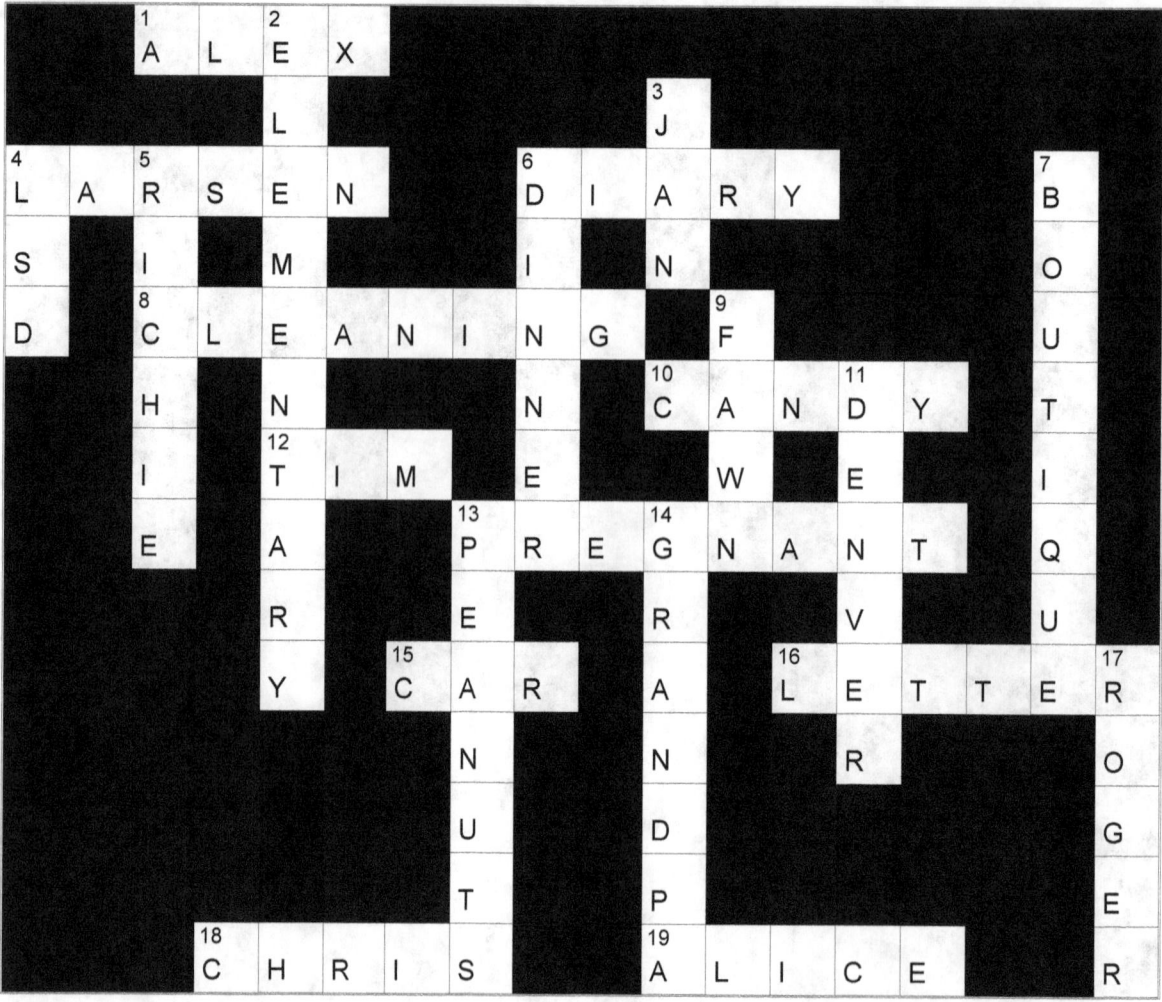

Across
1. Alice's younger sister
4. Last name of the family Alice babysits for
6. What Alice locks in a metal box
8. Alice has fun doing this with her family after a New Year's Eve party.
10. What Alice wants to put drugs on to get her younger brother to experience being high
12. Alice's younger brother
13. Because Alice is worried she is ___, she can't sleep, and the doctor prescribes tranquilizers.
15. Kids at school threaten to hide drugs in Alice's father's ___ to get him in trouble.
16. Joel sends Alice this while she is in the hospital.
18. Girl Alice runs away with
19. She wrote the diary and died.

Down
2. Alice is ashamed that she sells drugs at the ___ school.
3. Girl who shows up high while Alice is babysitting
4. Drug in Alice's Coke when she first took drugs
5. Name of boyfriend who got Alice into selling drugs
6. Alice makes this for her mother as a surprise for her birthday.
7. Kind of store Alice and Chris open
9. 'Straight' girl Alice becomes friends with
11. City Alice first goes to the second time she runs away
13. They were covered in acid, sending Alice on a bad trip ending with her going to the hospital.
14. He has a heart attack and dies.
17. Boy Alice really likes; he stands her up at the start of the book

Go Ask Alice Crossword 4

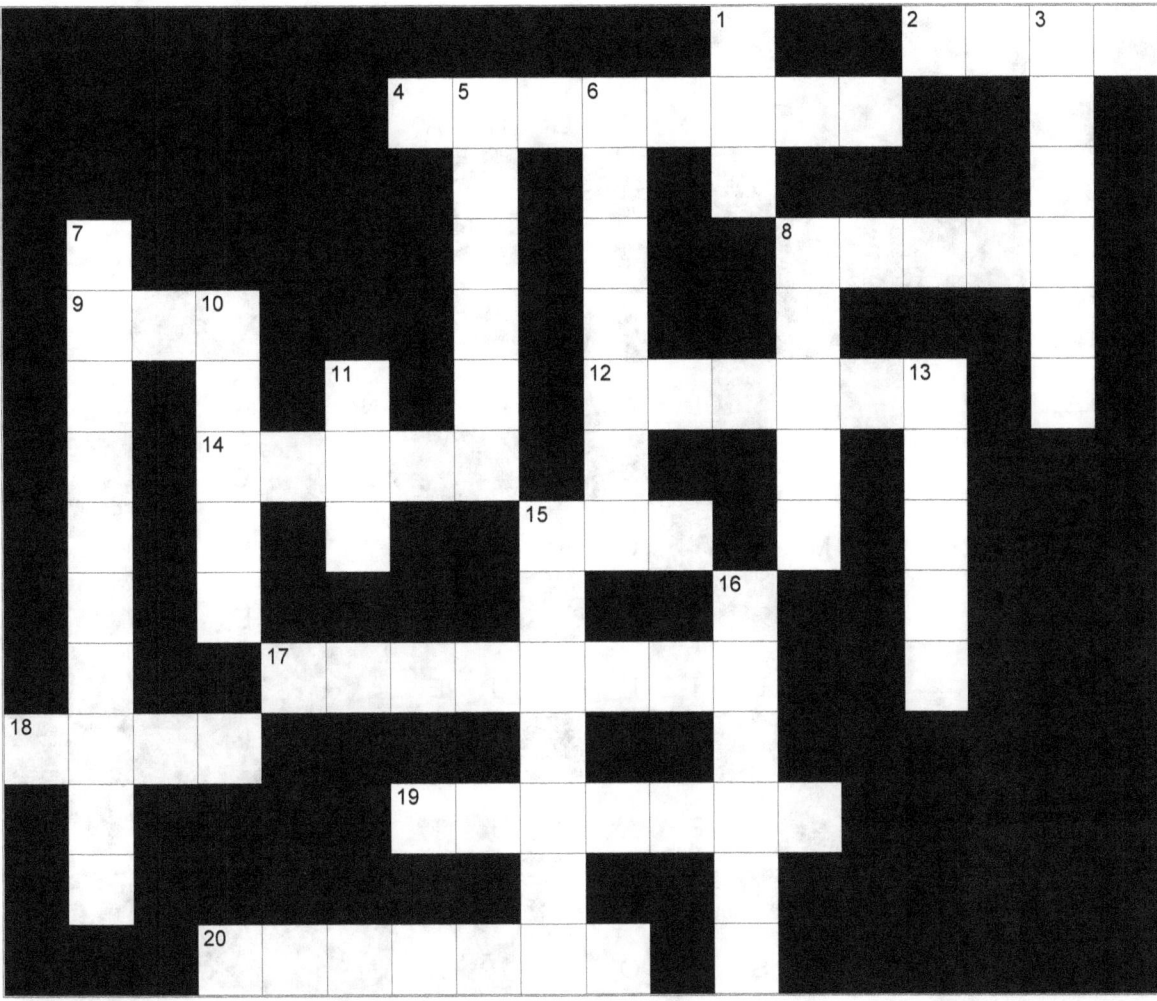

Across
2. Girl's house where Alice played 'Button, Button, Who's Got the Button?'
4. Because Alice is worried she is ___, she can't sleep, and the doctor prescribes tranquilizers.
8. Girl Alice runs away with
9. Drug in Alice's Coke when she first took drugs
12. Alice makes this for her mother as a surprise for her birthday.
14. She wrote the diary and died.
15. Kids at school threaten to hide drugs in Alice's father's ___ to get him in trouble.
17. Kind of store Alice and Chris open
18. 'Straight' girl Alice becomes friends with
19. They were covered in acid, sending Alice on a bad trip ending with her going to the hospital.
20. People who take Alice to the doctor & give her food & clothes

Down
1. Girl who shows up high while Alice is babysitting
3. Last name of the family Alice babysits for
5. Name of boyfriend who got Alice into selling drugs
6. He has a heart attack and dies.
7. Alice is ashamed that she sells drugs at the ___ school.
8. What Alice wants to put drugs on to get her younger brother to experience being high
10. What Alice locks in a metal box
11. Alice's younger brother
13. Boy Alice really likes; he stands her up at the start of the book
15. City where Joel lives
16. Joel sends Alice this while she is in the hospital.

Go Ask Alice Crossword 4 Answer Key

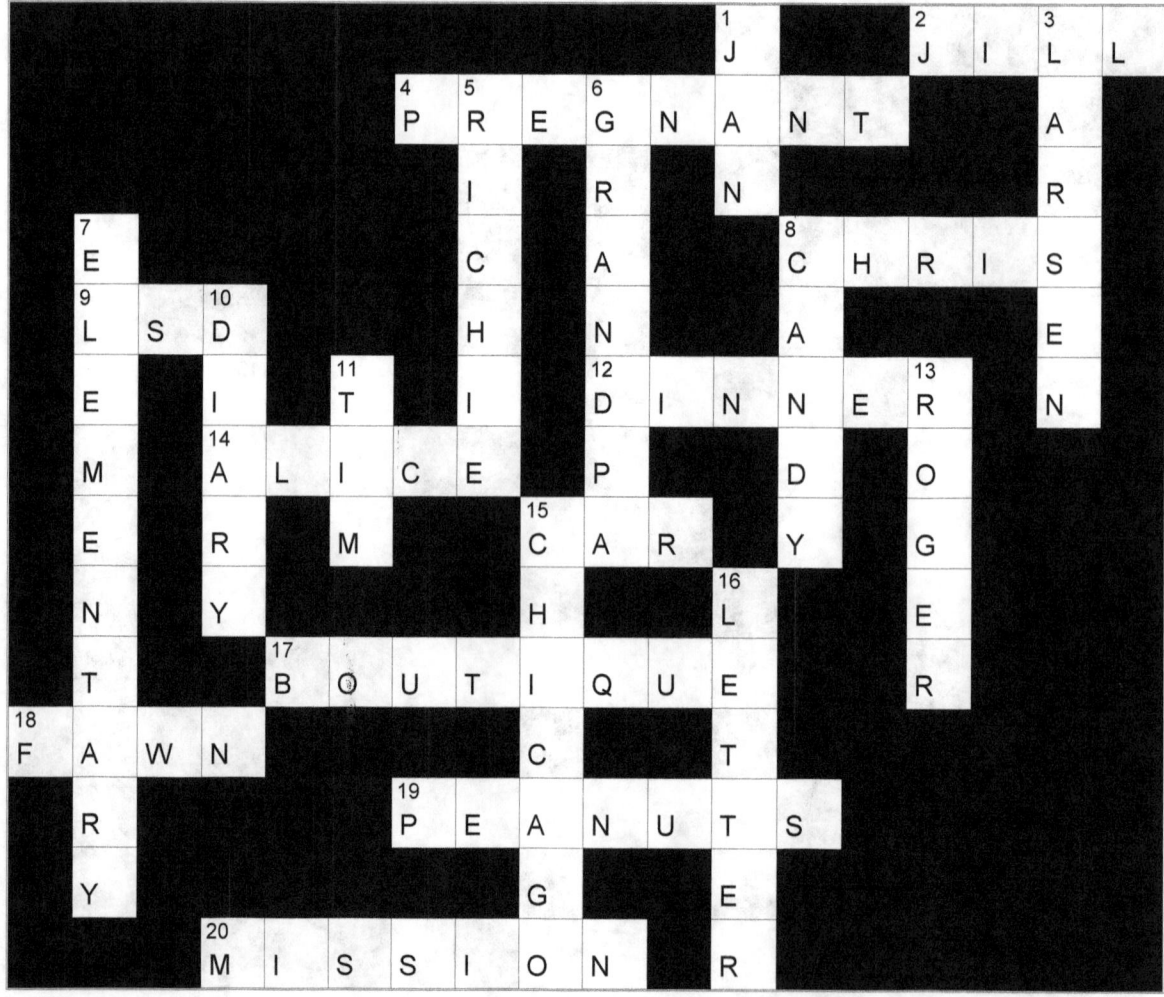

Across
2. Girl's house where Alice played 'Button, Button, Who's Got the Button?'
4. Because Alice is worried she is ___, she can't sleep, and the doctor prescribes tranquilizers.
8. Girl Alice runs away with
9. Drug in Alice's Coke when she first took drugs
12. Alice makes this for her mother as a surprise for her birthday.
14. She wrote the diary and died.
15. Kids at school threaten to hide drugs in Alice's father's ___ to get him in trouble.
17. Kind of store Alice and Chris open
18. 'Straight' girl Alice becomes friends with
19. They were covered in acid, sending Alice on a bad trip ending with her going to the hospital.
20. People who take Alice to the doctor & give her food & clothes

Down
1. Girl who shows up high while Alice is babysitting
3. Last name of the family Alice babysits for
5. Name of boyfriend who got Alice into selling drugs
6. He has a heart attack and dies.
7. Alice is ashamed that she sells drugs at the ___ school.
8. What Alice wants to put drugs on to get her younger brother to experience being high
10. What Alice locks in a metal box
11. Alice's younger brother
13. Boy Alice really likes; he stands her up at the start of the book
15. City where Joel lives
16. Joel sends Alice this while she is in the hospital.

Go Ask Alice

LSD	MOUNTAINS	GRANDMA	BOUTIQUE	TIM
BABBIE	MARCIE	CHICAGO	JILL	FAWN
LETTER	CAR	FREE SPACE	JAN	CHRIS
PIANO	ALEX	CANDY	HAPPINESS	PEANUTS
PROFESSOR	ROGER	RICHIE	CLEANING	MISSION

Go Ask Alice

GRANDPA	PREGNANT	LARSEN	DIARY	CHRISTMAS
JEWELRY	ALICE	DINNER	SHELIA	JOEL
DENVER	MISSION	FREE SPACE	RICHIE	ROGER
PROFESSOR	PEANUTS	HAPPINESS	CANDY	ALEX
PIANO	CHRIS	JAN	ELEMENTARY	CAR

Go Ask Alice

CANDY	LSD	JEWELRY	JAN	CAR
PREGNANT	HAPPINESS	JILL	MARCIE	BOUTIQUE
CLEANING	LETTER	FREE SPACE	JOEL	DINNER
GRANDMA	ELEMENTARY	ALEX	DENVER	GRANDPA
ALICE	PROFESSOR	PIANO	LARSEN	RICHIE

Go Ask Alice

CHRIS	SHELIA	PEANUTS	MOUNTAINS	FAWN
TIM	DIARY	BABBIE	CHRISTMAS	CHICAGO
ROGER	RICHIE	FREE SPACE	PIANO	PROFESSOR
ALICE	GRANDPA	DENVER	ALEX	ELEMENTARY
GRANDMA	DINNER	JOEL	MISSION	LETTER

Go Ask Alice

CHICAGO	TIM	DIARY	JAN	JEWELRY
JILL	ALEX	BABBIE	HAPPINESS	DINNER
PIANO	GRANDMA	FREE SPACE	LETTER	SHELIA
BOUTIQUE	RICHIE	MARCIE	MOUNTAINS	CAR
CHRISTMAS	CANDY	GRANDPA	PEANUTS	CLEANING

Go Ask Alice

ELEMENTARY	MISSION	JOEL	LSD	LARSEN
FAWN	PROFESSOR	ROGER	PREGNANT	DENVER
CHRIS	CLEANING	FREE SPACE	GRANDPA	CANDY
CHRISTMAS	CAR	MOUNTAINS	MARCIE	RICHIE
BOUTIQUE	SHELIA	LETTER	ALICE	GRANDMA

Go Ask Alice

GRANDMA	CHICAGO	BOUTIQUE	LETTER	JILL
CAR	JOEL	SHELIA	RICHIE	LSD
ROGER	MARCIE	FREE SPACE	MOUNTAINS	PEANUTS
JAN	ALICE	TIM	DIARY	LARSEN
JEWELRY	MISSION	PIANO	FAWN	CHRISTMAS

Go Ask Alice

PROFESSOR	DENVER	PREGNANT	ALEX	BABBIE
GRANDPA	DINNER	CHRIS	HAPPINESS	ELEMENTARY
CLEANING	CHRISTMAS	FREE SPACE	PIANO	MISSION
JEWELRY	LARSEN	DIARY	TIM	ALICE
JAN	PEANUTS	MOUNTAINS	CANDY	MARCIE

Go Ask Alice

HAPPINESS	BABBIE	DENVER	CHRIS	CLEANING
RICHIE	CHRISTMAS	JAN	JILL	PREGNANT
DINNER	CANDY	FREE SPACE	BOUTIQUE	ALEX
PROFESSOR	PIANO	MOUNTAINS	PEANUTS	GRANDPA
CHICAGO	DIARY	CAR	ELEMENTARY	JEWELRY

Go Ask Alice

MARCIE	LSD	FAWN	SHELIA	ALICE
LARSEN	ROGER	JOEL	GRANDMA	LETTER
TIM	JEWELRY	FREE SPACE	CAR	DIARY
CHICAGO	GRANDPA	PEANUTS	MOUNTAINS	PIANO
PROFESSOR	ALEX	BOUTIQUE	MISSION	CANDY

Go Ask Alice

JEWELRY	LARSEN	MISSION	CHRIS	BABBIE
RICHIE	ALICE	TIM	LSD	CHICAGO
ROGER	FAWN	FREE SPACE	ELEMENTARY	CLEANING
JOEL	PIANO	PEANUTS	MARCIE	JILL
DIARY	HAPPINESS	DINNER	GRANDMA	MOUNTAINS

Go Ask Alice

CAR	BOUTIQUE	LETTER	JAN	SHELIA
PROFESSOR	CHRISTMAS	CANDY	ALEX	DENVER
PREGNANT	MOUNTAINS	FREE SPACE	DINNER	HAPPINESS
DIARY	JILL	MARCIE	PEANUTS	PIANO
JOEL	CLEANING	ELEMENTARY	GRANDPA	FAWN

Go Ask Alice

LETTER	PROFESSOR	DIARY	LSD	CLEANING
JAN	PEANUTS	BABBIE	CHRISTMAS	JILL
ALICE	LARSEN	FREE SPACE	PREGNANT	CAR
PIANO	HAPPINESS	JOEL	TIM	CANDY
JEWELRY	ROGER	CHRIS	GRANDPA	BOUTIQUE

Go Ask Alice

MARCIE	MISSION	CHICAGO	ALEX	FAWN
ELEMENTARY	MOUNTAINS	RICHIE	SHELIA	DENVER
GRANDMA	BOUTIQUE	FREE SPACE	CHRIS	ROGER
JEWELRY	CANDY	TIM	JOEL	HAPPINESS
PIANO	CAR	PREGNANT	DINNER	LARSEN

Go Ask Alice

CLEANING	MOUNTAINS	CHICAGO	SHELIA	CANDY
MARCIE	JOEL	MISSION	BOUTIQUE	DENVER
HAPPINESS	TIM	FREE SPACE	PEANUTS	PROFESSOR
JILL	BABBIE	PREGNANT	DINNER	GRANDPA
FAWN	ELEMENTARY	CHRIS	LARSEN	ROGER

Go Ask Alice

DIARY	LSD	RICHIE	ALICE	LETTER
CHRISTMAS	JEWELRY	PIANO	GRANDMA	JAN
CAR	ROGER	FREE SPACE	CHRIS	ELEMENTARY
FAWN	GRANDPA	DINNER	PREGNANT	BABBIE
JILL	PROFESSOR	PEANUTS	ALEX	TIM

Go Ask Alice

CHRISTMAS	RICHIE	PREGNANT	GRANDPA	GRANDMA
MISSION	CANDY	CHICAGO	PEANUTS	BOUTIQUE
SHELIA	DINNER	FREE SPACE	PIANO	FAWN
ROGER	JAN	CLEANING	DIARY	LARSEN
DENVER	PROFESSOR	HAPPINESS	JOEL	JEWELRY

Go Ask Alice

CAR	MOUNTAINS	ELEMENTARY	BABBIE	ALEX
MARCIE	LETTER	CHRIS	ALICE	JILL
LSD	JEWELRY	FREE SPACE	HAPPINESS	PROFESSOR
DENVER	LARSEN	DIARY	CLEANING	JAN
ROGER	FAWN	PIANO	TIM	DINNER

Go Ask Alice

PROFESSOR	PIANO	MARCIE	CHRISTMAS	PREGNANT
JOEL	CHRIS	CHICAGO	GRANDPA	LSD
JEWELRY	MISSION	FREE SPACE	ALICE	MOUNTAINS
GRANDMA	FAWN	RICHIE	ELEMENTARY	DENVER
HAPPINESS	JAN	CAR	LARSEN	DINNER

Go Ask Alice

TIM	DIARY	CLEANING	BABBIE	LETTER
BOUTIQUE	SHELIA	JILL	ALEX	ROGER
PEANUTS	DINNER	FREE SPACE	CAR	JAN
HAPPINESS	DENVER	ELEMENTARY	RICHIE	FAWN
GRANDMA	MOUNTAINS	ALICE	CANDY	MISSION

Go Ask Alice

JAN	HAPPINESS	ALEX	JEWELRY	GRANDPA
DIARY	JOEL	MOUNTAINS	DENVER	LARSEN
ELEMENTARY	TIM	FREE SPACE	MISSION	GRANDMA
PIANO	JILL	PEANUTS	CANDY	CHRIS
RICHIE	CLEANING	SHELIA	LSD	MARCIE

Go Ask Alice

LETTER	CAR	BOUTIQUE	CHICAGO	BABBIE
DINNER	PROFESSOR	FAWN	ALICE	PREGNANT
ROGER	MARCIE	FREE SPACE	SHELIA	CLEANING
RICHIE	CHRIS	CANDY	PEANUTS	JILL
PIANO	GRANDMA	MISSION	CHRISTMAS	TIM

Go Ask Alice

GRANDMA	CAR	CLEANING	JAN	GRANDPA
PIANO	SHELIA	DIARY	DINNER	CHRISTMAS
JILL	LARSEN	FREE SPACE	ROGER	HAPPINESS
PREGNANT	FAWN	PROFESSOR	CANDY	CHICAGO
BOUTIQUE	PEANUTS	TIM	JEWELRY	BABBIE

Go Ask Alice

ALEX	DENVER	MISSION	JOEL	ELEMENTARY
LETTER	LSD	CHRIS	MOUNTAINS	ALICE
MARCIE	BABBIE	FREE SPACE	TIM	PEANUTS
BOUTIQUE	CHICAGO	CANDY	PROFESSOR	FAWN
PREGNANT	HAPPINESS	ROGER	RICHIE	LARSEN

Go Ask Alice

PREGNANT	ALEX	MARCIE	CHRISTMAS	BABBIE
JOEL	LETTER	ELEMENTARY	BOUTIQUE	MISSION
ALICE	DIARY	FREE SPACE	JAN	PIANO
CLEANING	PEANUTS	CANDY	CHICAGO	RICHIE
PROFESSOR	CHRIS	TIM	HAPPINESS	SHELIA

Go Ask Alice

LSD	FAWN	GRANDMA	JEWELRY	JILL
DENVER	LARSEN	DINNER	CAR	GRANDPA
MOUNTAINS	SHELIA	FREE SPACE	TIM	CHRIS
PROFESSOR	RICHIE	CHICAGO	CANDY	PEANUTS
CLEANING	PIANO	JAN	ROGER	DIARY

Go Ask Alice

LETTER	JAN	BABBIE	ROGER	CHICAGO
PIANO	MISSION	PROFESSOR	BOUTIQUE	SHELIA
MOUNTAINS	DINNER	FREE SPACE	CANDY	CAR
GRANDPA	GRANDMA	DENVER	CHRIS	HAPPINESS
LARSEN	FAWN	JOEL	MARCIE	JEWELRY

Go Ask Alice

ELEMENTARY	ALEX	RICHIE	PREGNANT	CLEANING
PEANUTS	LSD	JILL	DIARY	ALICE
TIM	JEWELRY	FREE SPACE	JOEL	FAWN
LARSEN	HAPPINESS	CHRIS	DENVER	GRANDMA
GRANDPA	CAR	CANDY	CHRISTMAS	DINNER

Go Ask Alice

CLEANING	JEWELRY	FAWN	CHICAGO	DINNER
LETTER	CAR	TIM	GRANDMA	JAN
GRANDPA	HAPPINESS	FREE SPACE	CHRIS	DENVER
JOEL	RICHIE	ROGER	MARCIE	DIARY
BABBIE	ELEMENTARY	CANDY	PIANO	CHRISTMAS

Go Ask Alice

MISSION	PROFESSOR	PREGNANT	PEANUTS	LSD
JILL	ALEX	MOUNTAINS	LARSEN	SHELIA
ALICE	CHRISTMAS	FREE SPACE	CANDY	ELEMENTARY
BABBIE	DIARY	MARCIE	ROGER	RICHIE
JOEL	DENVER	CHRIS	BOUTIQUE	HAPPINESS

Go Ask Alice

LARSEN	GRANDPA	FAWN	RICHIE	CANDY
JEWELRY	ROGER	SHELIA	ALEX	DINNER
PIANO	GRANDMA	FREE SPACE	LSD	JILL
BABBIE	PEANUTS	DENVER	CHICAGO	HAPPINESS
JAN	LETTER	CHRIS	CLEANING	JOEL

Go Ask Alice

TIM	PREGNANT	ALICE	MARCIE	CHRISTMAS
PROFESSOR	DIARY	CAR	BOUTIQUE	MOUNTAINS
ELEMENTARY	JOEL	FREE SPACE	CHRIS	LETTER
JAN	HAPPINESS	CHICAGO	DENVER	PEANUTS
BABBIE	JILL	LSD	MISSION	GRANDMA

Go Ask Alice Vocabulary Word List

No.	Word	Clue/Definition
1.	AFFIDAVIT	Written statement or declaration made under oath
2.	ANTAGONISTIC	Hostile; unfriendly
3.	ARTICULATE	Distinct, fluent, meaningful, and clear in the power of speech
4.	ASININE	Foolish; silly; stupid
5.	ASTRAY	Off or away from the correct or right path
6.	BLASE	Bored with life or unimpressed
7.	BLEARY	Blurred from sleep or fatigue; unclear
8.	CLODDY	Stupid or of lesser dignity or value
9.	CONCEIVE	Imagine; form an idea of
10.	CONSCIENTIOUS	Characterized by taking extreme care and/or making great effort
11.	CONTENTION	Disagreement; point of disagreement
12.	DEGENERATE	One who falls below the desirable level of quality
13.	DISCREET	Showing wise self-restraint in behavior
14.	DISDAIN	The feeling that someone or something is unworthy of one's consideration or respect
15.	DISSERTATION	Lengthy, formal speech or writing about a particular topic
16.	DISTINCTION	Recognizing or distinguishing differences
17.	ECHELON	Level of command, authority, or rank
18.	ENTITY	Something that exists as its own self or being
19.	FINK	Informer, spy, or someone who squeals
20.	FIRMAMENT	The expanse of the sky
21.	FOREBODING	Strong feeling of coming misfortune or evil
22.	FORTITUDE	Mental and emotional strength in facing difficulty
23.	GREGARIOUS	Seeking the company of others; outgoing and sociable
24.	IMPREGNABLE	Unable to be captured, overthrown, or broken into
25.	INFERIOR	Lower in position, rank, or worth
26.	INSCRIPTION	Marking of words or a message on an item
27.	INTERMINABLE	Unending
28.	LAMENTED	Expressed grief or regret; mourned
29.	LECHEROUS	Suggestive; lustful
30.	MONOPOLIZE	To have complete possession of; to dominate
31.	MUNDANE	Common; dull; boring; unimaginative
32.	NARY	Not any; no; never
33.	NONCHALANTLY	In a way cooly unconcerned, indifferent, or casual
34.	PENANCE	Act of devotion to pay for a sin or wrongdoing
35.	PERCEPTIVE	Understanding with insight or intuition
36.	PERSECUTING	Pursuing with harassment; annoying persistently
37.	PHENOMENA	Something that is remarkable, impressive, or extraordinary
38.	PREMONITIONS	Advance warnings of the future
39.	PRODIGAL	Wastefully extravagant
40.	PRYING	Looking at closely or curiously
41.	RAVINGS	Wild, delirious, or frenzied talking
42.	RECRIMINATIONS	Accusations in response to accusations from someone else
43.	REVELATION	Something that is uncovered, not previously known
44.	SIDLED	Edged or moved up sideways
45.	SIEGE	Assault; attack
46.	STIFLING	Smothering or suffocating
47.	TEEMING	Full of things; swarming
48.	TRANSGRESSIONS	Violations of laws or duties
49.	VACILLATING	Indecisive; unsteady; wavering
50.	VINDICTIVE	Revengeful; with the desire to hurt another

Go Ask Alice Vocabulary Fill In The Blanks 1

_____   1. Hostile; unfriendly

_____   2. Level of command, authority, or rank

_____   3. Informer, spy, or someone who squeals

_____   4. Distinct, fluent, meaningful, and clear in the power of speech

_____   5. Characterized by taking extreme care and/or making great effort

_____   6. Stupid or of lesser dignity or value

_____   7. The expanse of the sky

_____   8. Common; dull; boring; unimaginative

_____   9. Suggestive; lustful

_____   10. Pursuing with harassment; annoying persistently

_____   11. Accusations in response to accusations from someone else

_____   12. Wastefully extravagant

_____   13. Off or away from the correct or right path

_____   14. Edged or moved up sideways

_____   15. Advance warnings of the future

_____   16. Disagreement; point of disagreement

_____   17. Lower in position, rank, or worth

_____   18. Imagine; form an idea of

_____   19. Marking of words or a message on an item

_____   20. Something that is remarkable, impressive, or extraordinary

Go Ask Alice Vocabulary Fill In The Blanks 1 Answer Key

ANTAGONISTIC	1. Hostile; unfriendly
ECHELON	2. Level of command, authority, or rank
FINK	3. Informer, spy, or someone who squeals
ARTICULATE	4. Distinct, fluent, meaningful, and clear in the power of speech
CONSCIENTIOUS	5. Characterized by taking extreme care and/or making great effort
CLODDY	6. Stupid or of lesser dignity or value
FIRMAMENT	7. The expanse of the sky
MUNDANE	8. Common; dull; boring; unimaginative
LECHEROUS	9. Suggestive; lustful
PERSECUTING	10. Pursuing with harassment; annoying persistently
RECRIMINATIONS	11. Accusations in response to accusations from someone else
PRODIGAL	12. Wastefully extravagant
ASTRAY	13. Off or away from the correct or right path
SIDLED	14. Edged or moved up sideways
PREMONITIONS	15. Advance warnings of the future
CONTENTION	16. Disagreement; point of disagreement
INFERIOR	17. Lower in position, rank, or worth
CONCEIVE	18. Imagine; form an idea of
INSCRIPTION	19. Marking of words or a message on an item
PHENOMENA	20. Something that is remarkable, impressive, or extraordinary

Go Ask Alice Vocabulary Fill In The Blanks 2

_____ 1. Something that exists as its own self or being

_____ 2. Foolish; silly; stupid

_____ 3. Understanding with insight or intuition

_____ 4. Blurred from sleep or fatigue; unclear

_____ 5. Expressed grief or regret; mourned

_____ 6. Hostile; unfriendly

_____ 7. The expanse of the sky

_____ 8. Imagine; form an idea of

_____ 9. Something that is remarkable, impressive, or extraordinary

_____ 10. Lower in position, rank, or worth

_____ 11. Strong feeling of coming misfortune or evil

_____ 12. Act of devotion to pay for a sin or wrongdoing

_____ 13. Off or away from the correct or right path

_____ 14. Advance warnings of the future

_____ 15. Something that is uncovered, not previously known

_____ 16. The feeling that someone or something is unworthy of one's consideration or respect

_____ 17. Mental and emotional strength in facing difficulty

_____ 18. Stupid or of lesser dignity or value

_____ 19. Smothering or suffocating

_____ 20. Violations of laws or duties

Go Ask Alice Vocabulary Fill In The Blanks 2 Answer Key

ENTITY	1. Something that exists as its own self or being
ASININE	2. Foolish; silly; stupid
PERCEPTIVE	3. Understanding with insight or intuition
BLEARY	4. Blurred from sleep or fatigue; unclear
LAMENTED	5. Expressed grief or regret; mourned
ANTAGONISTIC	6. Hostile; unfriendly
FIRMAMENT	7. The expanse of the sky
CONCEIVE	8. Imagine; form an idea of
PHENOMENA	9. Something that is remarkable, impressive, or extraordinary
INFERIOR	10. Lower in position, rank, or worth
FOREBODING	11. Strong feeling of coming misfortune or evil
PENANCE	12. Act of devotion to pay for a sin or wrongdoing
ASTRAY	13. Off or away from the correct or right path
PREMONITIONS	14. Advance warnings of the future
REVELATION	15. Something that is uncovered, not previously known
DISDAIN	16. The feeling that someone or something is unworthy of one's consideration or respect
FORTITUDE	17. Mental and emotional strength in facing difficulty
CLODDY	18. Stupid or of lesser dignity or value
STIFLING	19. Smothering or suffocating
TRANSGRESSIONS	20. Violations of laws or duties

Go Ask Alice Vocabulary Fill In The Blanks 3

_____ 1. Full of things; swarming

_____ 2. Not any; no; never

_____ 3. Level of command, authority, or rank

_____ 4. Blurred from sleep or fatigue; unclear

_____ 5. Foolish; silly; stupid

_____ 6. Violations of laws or duties

_____ 7. Characterized by taking extreme care and/or making great effort

_____ 8. Indecisive; unsteady; wavering

_____ 9. Recognizing or distinguishing differences

_____ 10. Act of devotion to pay for a sin or wrongdoing

_____ 11. Smothering or suffocating

_____ 12. One who falls below the desirable level of quality

_____ 13. Unending

_____ 14. Unable to be captured, overthrown, or broken into

_____ 15. Edged or moved up sideways

_____ 16. Something that is remarkable, impressive, or extraordinary

_____ 17. Disagreement; point of disagreement

_____ 18. Assault; attack

_____ 19. Written statement or declaration made under oath

_____ 20. Understanding with insight or intuition

Go Ask Alice Vocabulary Fill In The Blanks 3 Answer Key

TEEMING	1. Full of things; swarming
NARY	2. Not any; no; never
ECHELON	3. Level of command, authority, or rank
BLEARY	4. Blurred from sleep or fatigue; unclear
ASININE	5. Foolish; silly; stupid
TRANSGRESSIONS	6. Violations of laws or duties
CONSCIENTIOUS	7. Characterized by taking extreme care and/or making great effort
VACILLATING	8. Indecisive; unsteady; wavering
DISTINCTION	9. Recognizing or distinguishing differences
PENANCE	10. Act of devotion to pay for a sin or wrongdoing
STIFLING	11. Smothering or suffocating
DEGENERATE	12. One who falls below the desirable level of quality
INTERMINABLE	13. Unending
IMPREGNABLE	14. Unable to be captured, overthrown, or broken into
SIDLED	15. Edged or moved up sideways
PHENOMENA	16. Something that is remarkable, impressive, or extraordinary
CONTENTION	17. Disagreement; point of disagreement
SIEGE	18. Assault; attack
AFFIDAVIT	19. Written statement or declaration made under oath
PERCEPTIVE	20. Understanding with insight or intuition

Go Ask Alice Vocabulary Fill In The Blanks 4

_____ 1. Indecisive; unsteady; wavering

_____ 2. Something that is uncovered, not previously known

_____ 3. Full of things; swarming

_____ 4. In a way cooly unconcerned, indifferent, or casual

_____ 5. Not any; no; never

_____ 6. Lower in position, rank, or worth

_____ 7. Blurred from sleep or fatigue; unclear

_____ 8. Understanding with insight or intuition

_____ 9. Something that exists as its own self or being

_____ 10. To have complete possession of; to dominate

_____ 11. Level of command, authority, or rank

_____ 12. Assault; attack

_____ 13. Mental and emotional strength in facing difficulty

_____ 14. Distinct, fluent, meaningful, and clear in the power of speech

_____ 15. Smothering or suffocating

_____ 16. Unable to be captured, overthrown, or broken into

_____ 17. Recognizing or distinguishing differences

_____ 18. Wild, delirious, or frenzied talking

_____ 19. Characterized by taking extreme care and/or making great effort

_____ 20. Lengthy, formal speech or writing about a particular topic

Go Ask Alice Vocabulary Fill In The Blanks 4 Answer Key

VACILLATING	1. Indecisive; unsteady; wavering
REVELATION	2. Something that is uncovered, not previously known
TEEMING	3. Full of things; swarming
NONCHALANTLY	4. In a way cooly unconcerned, indifferent, or casual
NARY	5. Not any; no; never
INFERIOR	6. Lower in position, rank, or worth
BLEARY	7. Blurred from sleep or fatigue; unclear
PERCEPTIVE	8. Understanding with insight or intuition
ENTITY	9. Something that exists as its own self or being
MONOPOLIZE	10. To have complete possession of; to dominate
ECHELON	11. Level of command, authority, or rank
SIEGE	12. Assault; attack
FORTITUDE	13. Mental and emotional strength in facing difficulty
ARTICULATE	14. Distinct, fluent, meaningful, and clear in the power of speech
STIFLING	15. Smothering or suffocating
IMPREGNABLE	16. Unable to be captured, overthrown, or broken into
DISTINCTION	17. Recognizing or distinguishing differences
RAVINGS	18. Wild, delirious, or frenzied talking
CONSCIENTIOUS	19. Characterized by taking extreme care and/or making great effort
DISSERTATION	20. Lengthy, formal speech or writing about a particular topic

Go Ask Alice Vocabulary Matching 1

___ 1. CONSCIENTIOUS   A. To have complete possession of; to dominate
___ 2. VINDICTIVE   B. Characterized by taking extreme care and/or making great effort
___ 3. GREGARIOUS   C. Indecisive; unsteady; wavering
___ 4. ARTICULATE   D. Revengeful; with the desire to hurt another
___ 5. DISSERTATION   E. Hostile; unfriendly
___ 6. INTERMINABLE   F. Lengthy, formal speech or writing about a particular topic
___ 7. RAVINGS   G. Something that is uncovered, not previously known
___ 8. DISTINCTION   H. Disagreement; point of disagreement
___ 9. ANTAGONISTIC   I. Informer, spy, or someone who squeals
___10. VACILLATING   J. Seeking the company of others; outgoing and sociable
___11. RECRIMINATIONS   K. Assault; attack
___12. SIEGE   L. Distinct, fluent, meaningful, and clear in the power of speech
___13. SIDLED   M. In a way cooly unconcerned, indifferent, or casual
___14. TEEMING   N. Accusations in response to accusations from someone else
___15. FINK   O. Recognizing or distinguishing differences
___16. CONTENTION   P. Unending
___17. FORTITUDE   Q. Mental and emotional strength in facing difficulty
___18. MUNDANE   R. Blurred from sleep or fatigue; unclear
___19. MONOPOLIZE   S. Understanding with insight or intuition
___20. PERCEPTIVE   T. Edged or moved up sideways
___21. ASININE   U. Off or away from the correct or right path
___22. ASTRAY   V. Common; dull; boring; unimaginative
___23. NONCHALANTLY   W. Foolish; silly; stupid
___24. BLEARY   X. Wild, delirious, or frenzied talking
___25. REVELATION   Y. Full of things; swarming

Go Ask Alice Vocabulary Matching 1 Answer Key

B - 1.	CONSCIENTIOUS	A. To have complete possession of; to dominate
D - 2.	VINDICTIVE	B. Characterized by taking extreme care and/or making great effort
J - 3.	GREGARIOUS	C. Indecisive; unsteady; wavering
L - 4.	ARTICULATE	D. Revengeful; with the desire to hurt another
F - 5.	DISSERTATION	E. Hostile; unfriendly
P - 6.	INTERMINABLE	F. Lengthy, formal speech or writing about a particular topic
X - 7.	RAVINGS	G. Something that is uncovered, not previously known
O - 8.	DISTINCTION	H. Disagreement; point of disagreement
E - 9.	ANTAGONISTIC	I. Informer, spy, or someone who squeals
C - 10.	VACILLATING	J. Seeking the company of others; outgoing and sociable
N - 11.	RECRIMINATIONS	K. Assault; attack
K - 12.	SIEGE	L. Distinct, fluent, meaningful, and clear in the power of speech
T - 13.	SIDLED	M. In a way cooly unconcerned, indifferent, or casual
Y - 14.	TEEMING	N. Accusations in response to accusations from someone else
I - 15.	FINK	O. Recognizing or distinguishing differences
H - 16.	CONTENTION	P. Unending
Q - 17.	FORTITUDE	Q. Mental and emotional strength in facing difficulty
V - 18.	MUNDANE	R. Blurred from sleep or fatigue; unclear
A - 19.	MONOPOLIZE	S. Understanding with insight or intuition
S - 20.	PERCEPTIVE	T. Edged or moved up sideways
W - 21.	ASININE	U. Off or away from the correct or right path
U - 22.	ASTRAY	V. Common; dull; boring; unimaginative
M - 23.	NONCHALANTLY	W. Foolish; silly; stupid
R - 24.	BLEARY	X. Wild, delirious, or frenzied talking
G - 25.	REVELATION	Y. Full of things; swarming

Go Ask Alice Vocabulary Matching 2

___ 1. PHENOMENA   A. Bored with life or unimpressed
___ 2. GREGARIOUS   B. Blurred from sleep or fatigue; unclear
___ 3. DISCREET   C. Common; dull; boring; unimaginative
___ 4. REVELATION   D. Unable to be captured, overthrown, or broken into
___ 5. DEGENERATE   E. Mental and emotional strength in facing difficulty
___ 6. NONCHALANTLY   F. Understanding with insight or intuition
___ 7. CLODDY   G. Revengeful; with the desire to hurt another
___ 8. TEEMING   H. Stupid or of lesser dignity or value
___ 9. FORTITUDE   I. In a way cooly unconcerned, indifferent, or casual
___10. BLASE   J. To have complete possession of; to dominate
___11. INSCRIPTION   K. One who falls below the desirable level of quality
___12. INTERMINABLE   L. Showing wise self-restraint in behavior
___13. ASTRAY   M. Something that is remarkable, impressive, or extraordinary
___14. PERCEPTIVE   N. The expanse of the sky
___15. IMPREGNABLE   O. Off or away from the correct or right path
___16. CONSCIENTIOUS   P. Unending
___17. MUNDANE   Q. Marking of words or a message on an item
___18. ASININE   R. Seeking the company of others; outgoing and sociable
___19. FIRMAMENT   S. Characterized by taking extreme care and/or making great effort
___20. SIDLED   T. Accusations in response to accusations from someone else
___21. CONCEIVE   U. Something that is uncovered, not previously known
___22. RECRIMINATIONS   V. Full of things; swarming
___23. VINDICTIVE   W. Edged or moved up sideways
___24. BLEARY   X. Foolish; silly; stupid
___25. MONOPOLIZE   Y. Imagine; form an idea of

Go Ask Alice Vocabulary Matching 2 Answer Key

M - 1.	PHENOMENA	A. Bored with life or unimpressed
R - 2.	GREGARIOUS	B. Blurred from sleep or fatigue; unclear
L - 3.	DISCREET	C. Common; dull; boring; unimaginative
U - 4.	REVELATION	D. Unable to be captured, overthrown, or broken into
K - 5.	DEGENERATE	E. Mental and emotional strength in facing difficulty
I - 6.	NONCHALANTLY	F. Understanding with insight or intuition
H - 7.	CLODDY	G. Revengeful; with the desire to hurt another
V - 8.	TEEMING	H. Stupid or of lesser dignity or value
E - 9.	FORTITUDE	I. In a way cooly unconcerned, indifferent, or casual
A - 10.	BLASE	J. To have complete possession of; to dominate
Q - 11.	INSCRIPTION	K. One who falls below the desirable level of quality
P - 12.	INTERMINABLE	L. Showing wise self-restraint in behavior
O - 13.	ASTRAY	M. Something that is remarkable, impressive, or extraordinary
F - 14.	PERCEPTIVE	N. The expanse of the sky
D - 15.	IMPREGNABLE	O. Off or away from the correct or right path
S - 16.	CONSCIENTIOUS	P. Unending
C - 17.	MUNDANE	Q. Marking of words or a message on an item
X - 18.	ASININE	R. Seeking the company of others; outgoing and sociable
N - 19.	FIRMAMENT	S. Characterized by taking extreme care and/or making great effort
W - 20.	SIDLED	T. Accusations in response to accusations from someone else
Y - 21.	CONCEIVE	U. Something that is uncovered, not previously known
T - 22.	RECRIMINATIONS	V. Full of things; swarming
G - 23.	VINDICTIVE	W. Edged or moved up sideways
B - 24.	BLEARY	X. Foolish; silly; stupid
J - 25.	MONOPOLIZE	Y. Imagine; form an idea of

Go Ask Alice Vocabulary Matching 3

___ 1. BLEARY
___ 2. DEGENERATE
___ 3. ARTICULATE
___ 4. DISDAIN
___ 5. PERSECUTING
___ 6. PERCEPTIVE
___ 7. INSCRIPTION
___ 8. ENTITY
___ 9. AFFIDAVIT
___ 10. CONSCIENTIOUS
___ 11. PHENOMENA
___ 12. REVELATION
___ 13. PRODIGAL
___ 14. NONCHALANTLY
___ 15. SIEGE
___ 16. TEEMING
___ 17. IMPREGNABLE
___ 18. ASININE
___ 19. CONCEIVE
___ 20. ANTAGONISTIC
___ 21. NARY
___ 22. DISSERTATION
___ 23. LECHEROUS
___ 24. ASTRAY
___ 25. LAMENTED

A. Written statement or declaration made under oath
B. Full of things; swarming
C. Imagine; form an idea of
D. Hostile; unfriendly
E. Wastefully extravagant
F. Blurred from sleep or fatigue; unclear
G. Unable to be captured, overthrown, or broken into
H. Lengthy, formal speech or writing about a particular topic
I. Not any; no; never
J. Expressed grief or regret; mourned
K. Pursuing with harassment; annoying persistently
L. Something that exists as its own self or being
M. Characterized by taking extreme care and/or making great effort
N. Suggestive; lustful
O. Something that is remarkable, impressive, or extraordinary
P. One who falls below the desirable level of quality
Q. Off or away from the correct or right path
R. Foolish; silly; stupid
S. In a way cooly unconcerned, indifferent, or casual
T. The feeling that someone or something is unworthy of one's consideration or respect
U. Something that is uncovered, not previously known
V. Understanding with insight or intuition
W. Marking of words or a message on an item
X. Assault; attack
Y. Distinct, fluent, meaningful, and clear in the power of speech

Go Ask Alice Vocabulary Matching 3 Answer Key

F - 1. BLEARY
P - 2. DEGENERATE
Y - 3. ARTICULATE
T - 4. DISDAIN
K - 5. PERSECUTING
V - 6. PERCEPTIVE
W - 7. INSCRIPTION
L - 8. ENTITY
A - 9. AFFIDAVIT
M - 10. CONSCIENTIOUS
O - 11. PHENOMENA
U - 12. REVELATION
E - 13. PRODIGAL
S - 14. NONCHALANTLY
X - 15. SIEGE
B - 16. TEEMING
G - 17. IMPREGNABLE
R - 18. ASININE
C - 19. CONCEIVE
D - 20. ANTAGONISTIC
I - 21. NARY
H - 22. DISSERTATION
N - 23. LECHEROUS
Q - 24. ASTRAY
J - 25. LAMENTED

A. Written statement or declaration made under oath
B. Full of things; swarming
C. Imagine; form an idea of
D. Hostile; unfriendly
E. Wastefully extravagant
F. Blurred from sleep or fatigue; unclear
G. Unable to be captured, overthrown, or broken into
H. Lengthy, formal speech or writing about a particular topic
I. Not any; no; never
J. Expressed grief or regret; mourned
K. Pursuing with harassment; annoying persistently
L. Something that exists as its own self or being
M. Characterized by taking extreme care and/or making great effort
N. Suggestive; lustful
O. Something that is remarkable, impressive, or extraordinary
P. One who falls below the desirable level of quality
Q. Off or away from the correct or right path
R. Foolish; silly; stupid
S. In a way cooly unconcerned, indifferent, or casual
T. The feeling that someone or something is unworthy of one's consideration or respect
U. Something that is uncovered, not previously known
V. Understanding with insight or intuition
W. Marking of words or a message on an item
X. Assault; attack
Y. Distinct, fluent, meaningful, and clear in the power of speech

Go Ask Alice Vocabulary Matching 4

___ 1. ASININE
___ 2. PRODIGAL
___ 3. DISSERTATION
___ 4. PHENOMENA
___ 5. INTERMINABLE
___ 6. LECHEROUS
___ 7. INFERIOR
___ 8. FINK
___ 9. PERSECUTING
___ 10. FIRMAMENT
___ 11. BLEARY
___ 12. LAMENTED
___ 13. MONOPOLIZE
___ 14. ECHELON
___ 15. ARTICULATE
___ 16. CONTENTION
___ 17. INSCRIPTION
___ 18. CONCEIVE
___ 19. TEEMING
___ 20. DISTINCTION
___ 21. AFFIDAVIT
___ 22. REVELATION
___ 23. ANTAGONISTIC
___ 24. IMPREGNABLE
___ 25. VINDICTIVE

A. Distinct, fluent, meaningful, and clear in the power of speech
B. Expressed grief or regret; mourned
C. Blurred from sleep or fatigue; unclear
D. Informer, spy, or someone who squeals
E. Disagreement; point of disagreement
F. Wastefully extravagant
G. Lower in position, rank, or worth
H. To have complete possession of; to dominate
I. Something that is remarkable, impressive, or extraordinary
J. Level of command, authority, or rank
K. Something that is uncovered, not previously known
L. Written statement or declaration made under oath
M. Pursuing with harassment; annoying persistently
N. Suggestive; lustful
O. Revengeful; with the desire to hurt another
P. Unending
Q. Lengthy, formal speech or writing about a particular topic
R. Marking of words or a message on an item
S. Imagine; form an idea of
T. Unable to be captured, overthrown, or broken into
U. Full of things; swarming
V. Hostile; unfriendly
W. Foolish; silly; stupid
X. Recognizing or distinguishing differences
Y. The expanse of the sky

Go Ask Alice Vocabulary Matching 4 Answer Key

W - 1.	ASININE	A.	Distinct, fluent, meaningful, and clear in the power of speech
F - 2.	PRODIGAL	B.	Expressed grief or regret; mourned
Q - 3.	DISSERTATION	C.	Blurred from sleep or fatigue; unclear
I - 4.	PHENOMENA	D.	Informer, spy, or someone who squeals
P - 5.	INTERMINABLE	E.	Disagreement; point of disagreement
N - 6.	LECHEROUS	F.	Wastefully extravagant
G - 7.	INFERIOR	G.	Lower in position, rank, or worth
D - 8.	FINK	H.	To have complete possession of; to dominate
M - 9.	PERSECUTING	I.	Something that is remarkable, impressive, or extraordinary
Y - 10.	FIRMAMENT	J.	Level of command, authority, or rank
C - 11.	BLEARY	K.	Something that is uncovered, not previously known
B - 12.	LAMENTED	L.	Written statement or declaration made under oath
H - 13.	MONOPOLIZE	M.	Pursuing with harassment; annoying persistently
J - 14.	ECHELON	N.	Suggestive; lustful
A - 15.	ARTICULATE	O.	Revengeful; with the desire to hurt another
E - 16.	CONTENTION	P.	Unending
R - 17.	INSCRIPTION	Q.	Lengthy, formal speech or writing about a particular topic
S - 18.	CONCEIVE	R.	Marking of words or a message on an item
U - 19.	TEEMING	S.	Imagine; form an idea of
X - 20.	DISTINCTION	T.	Unable to be captured, overthrown, or broken into
L - 21.	AFFIDAVIT	U.	Full of things; swarming
K - 22.	REVELATION	V.	Hostile; unfriendly
V - 23.	ANTAGONISTIC	W.	Foolish; silly; stupid
T - 24.	IMPREGNABLE	X.	Recognizing or distinguishing differences
O - 25.	VINDICTIVE	Y.	The expanse of the sky

Go Ask Alice Vocabulary Magic Squares 1

Match the definition with the vocabulary word. Put your answers in the magic squares below. When your answers are correct, all columns and rows will add to the same number.

A. DISDAIN
B. FOREBODING
C. PRYING
D. CONTENTION
E. SIEGE
F. FIRMAMENT
G. PENANCE
H. INSCRIPTION
I. IMPREGNABLE
J. GREGARIOUS
K. ASTRAY
L. CONCEIVE
M. BLASE
N. NARY
O. DISSERTATION
P. ECHELON

1. The expanse of the sky
2. Unable to be captured, overthrown, or broken into
3. Lengthy, formal speech or writing about a particular topic
4. Disagreement; point of disagreement
5. Bored with life or unimpressed
6. Strong feeling of coming misfortune or evil
7. Marking of words or a message on an item
8. Off or away from the correct or right path
9. Looking at closely or curiously
10. Level of command, authority, or rank
11. Seeking the company of others; outgoing and sociable
12. Assault; attack
13. Imagine; form an idea of
14. Act of devotion to pay for a sin or wrongdoing
15. The feeling that someone or something is unworthy of one's consideration or respect
16. Not any; no; never

A=	B=	C=	D=
E=	F=	G=	H=
I=	J=	K=	L=
M=	N=	O=	P=

Go Ask Alice Vocabulary Magic Squares 1 Answer Key

Match the definition with the vocabulary word. Put your answers in the magic squares below. When your answers are correct, all columns and rows will add to the same number.

A. DISDAIN
B. FOREBODING
C. PRYING
D. CONTENTION
E. SIEGE
F. FIRMAMENT
G. PENANCE
H. INSCRIPTION
I. IMPREGNABLE
J. GREGARIOUS
K. ASTRAY
L. CONCEIVE
M. BLASE
N. NARY
O. DISSERTATION
P. ECHELON

1. The expanse of the sky
2. Unable to be captured, overthrown, or broken into
3. Lengthy, formal speech or writing about a particular topic
4. Disagreement; point of disagreement
5. Bored with life or unimpressed
6. Strong feeling of coming misfortune or evil
7. Marking of words or a message on an item
8. Off or away from the correct or right path
9. Looking at closely or curiously
10. Level of command, authority, or rank
11. Seeking the company of others; outgoing and sociable
12. Assault; attack
13. Imagine; form an idea of
14. Act of devotion to pay for a sin or wrongdoing
15. The feeling that someone or something is unworthy of one's consideration or respect
16. Not any; no; never

A=15	B=6	C=9	D=4
E=12	F=1	G=14	H=7
I=2	J=11	K=8	L=13
M=5	N=16	O=3	P=10

Go Ask Alice Vocabulary Magic Squares 2

Match the definition with the vocabulary word. Put your answers in the magic squares below. When your answers are correct, all columns and rows will add to the same number.

A. IMPREGNABLE
B. NONCHALANTLY
C. DISSERTATION
D. VACILLATING
E. RAVINGS
F. STIFLING
G. AFFIDAVIT
H. CONTENTION
I. PRODIGAL
J. INTERMINABLE
K. VINDICTIVE
L. PENANCE
M. DEGENERATE
N. REVELATION
O. SIDLED
P. ECHELON

1. Unable to be captured, overthrown, or broken into
2. Something that is uncovered, not previously known
3. Unending
4. Wild, delirious, or frenzied talking
5. Written statement or declaration made under oath
6. Act of devotion to pay for a sin or wrongdoing
7. Level of command, authority, or rank
8. Lengthy, formal speech or writing about a particular topic
9. Edged or moved up sideways
10. Indecisive; unsteady; wavering
11. Disagreement; point of disagreement
12. Revengeful; with the desire to hurt another
13. Wastefully extravagant
14. Smothering or suffocating
15. In a way cooly unconcerned, indifferent, or casual
16. One who falls below the desirable level of quality

A=	B=	C=	D=
E=	F=	G=	H=
I=	J=	K=	L=
M=	N=	O=	P=

Go Ask Alice Vocabulary Magic Squares 2 Answer Key

Match the definition with the vocabulary word. Put your answers in the magic squares below. When your answers are correct, all columns and rows will add to the same number.

A. IMPREGNABLE
B. NONCHALANTLY
C. DISSERTATION
D. VACILLATING
E. RAVINGS
F. STIFLING
G. AFFIDAVIT
H. CONTENTION
I. PRODIGAL
J. INTERMINABLE
K. VINDICTIVE
L. PENANCE
M. DEGENERATE
N. REVELATION
O. SIDLED
P. ECHELON

1. Unable to be captured, overthrown, or broken into
2. Something that is uncovered, not previously known
3. Unending
4. Wild, delirious, or frenzied talking
5. Written statement or declaration made under oath
6. Act of devotion to pay for a sin or wrongdoing
7. Level of command, authority, or rank
8. Lengthy, formal speech or writing about a particular topic
9. Edged or moved up sideways
10. Indecisive; unsteady; wavering
11. Disagreement; point of disagreement
12. Revengeful; with the desire to hurt another
13. Wastefully extravagant
14. Smothering or suffocating
15. In a way cooly unconcerned, indifferent, or casual
16. One who falls below the desirable level of quality

A=1	B=15	C=8	D=10
E=4	F=14	G=5	H=11
I=13	J=3	K=12	L=6
M=16	N=2	O=9	P=7

Go Ask Alice Vocabulary Magic Squares 3

Match the definition with the vocabulary word. Put your answers in the magic squares below. When your answers are correct, all columns and rows will add to the same number.

A. BLEARY
B. ASININE
C. CONCEIVE
D. MUNDANE
E. CONSCIENTIOUS
F. IMPREGNABLE
G. ARTICULATE
H. FIRMAMENT
I. FINK
J. BLASE
K. INFERIOR
L. CONTENTION
M. PHENOMENA
N. INTERMINABLE
O. CLODDY
P. ANTAGONISTIC

1. The expanse of the sky
2. Blurred from sleep or fatigue; unclear
3. Foolish; silly; stupid
4. Distinct, fluent, meaningful, and clear in the power of speech
5. Bored with life or unimpressed
6. Stupid or of lesser dignity or value
7. Hostile; unfriendly
8. Informer, spy, or someone who squeals
9. Lower in position, rank, or worth
10. Unending
11. Something that is remarkable, impressive, or extraordinary
12. Disagreement; point of disagreement
13. Characterized by taking extreme care and/or making great effort
14. Common; dull; boring; unimaginative
15. Imagine; form an idea of
16. Unable to be captured, overthrown, or broken into

A=	B=	C=	D=
E=	F=	G=	H=
I=	J=	K=	L=
M=	N=	O=	P=

Go Ask Alice Vocabulary Magic Squares 3 Answer Key

Match the definition with the vocabulary word. Put your answers in the magic squares below. When your answers are correct, all columns and rows will add to the same number.

A. BLEARY
B. ASININE
C. CONCEIVE
D. MUNDANE
E. CONSCIENTIOUS
F. IMPREGNABLE
G. ARTICULATE
H. FIRMAMENT
I. FINK
J. BLASE
K. INFERIOR
L. CONTENTION
M. PHENOMENA
N. INTERMINABLE
O. CLODDY
P. ANTAGONISTIC

1. The expanse of the sky
2. Blurred from sleep or fatigue; unclear
3. Foolish; silly; stupid
4. Distinct, fluent, meaningful, and clear in the power of speech
5. Bored with life or unimpressed
6. Stupid or of lesser dignity or value
7. Hostile; unfriendly
8. Informer, spy, or someone who squeals
9. Lower in position, rank, or worth
10. Unending
11. Something that is remarkable, impressive, or extraordinary
12. Disagreement; point of disagreement
13. Characterized by taking extreme care and/or making great effort
14. Common; dull; boring; unimaginative
15. Imagine; form an idea of
16. Unable to be captured, overthrown, or broken into

A=2	B=3	C=15	D=14
E=13	F=16	G=4	H=1
I=8	J=5	K=9	L=12
M=11	N=10	O=6	P=7

Go Ask Alice Vocabulary Magic Squares 4

Match the definition with the vocabulary word. Put your answers in the magic squares below. When your answers are correct, all columns and rows will add to the same number.

A. DISSERTATION
B. STIFLING
C. MONOPOLIZE
D. INTERMINABLE
E. TEEMING
F. FOREBODING
G. ASININE
H. ECHELON
I. PREMONITIONS
J. PRODIGAL
K. SIEGE
L. PENANCE
M. NONCHALANTLY
N. ARTICULATE
O. CONCEIVE
P. AFFIDAVIT

1. Imagine; form an idea of
2. Unending
3. Wastefully extravagant
4. Full of things; swarming
5. Advance warnings of the future
6. Strong feeling of coming misfortune or evil
7. Written statement or declaration made under oath
8. To have complete possession of; to dominate
9. Level of command, authority, or rank
10. Assault; attack
11. Lengthy, formal speech or writing about a particular topic
12. Distinct, fluent, meaningful, and clear in the power of speech
13. Smothering or suffocating
14. In a way cooly unconcerned, indifferent, or casual
15. Foolish; silly; stupid
16. Act of devotion to pay for a sin or wrongdoing

A=	B=	C=	D=
E=	F=	G=	H=
I=	J=	K=	L=
M=	N=	O=	P=

Go Ask Alice Vocabulary Magic Squares 4 Answer Key

Match the definition with the vocabulary word. Put your answers in the magic squares below. When your answers are correct, all columns and rows will add to the same number.

A. DISSERTATION
B. STIFLING
C. MONOPOLIZE
D. INTERMINABLE
E. TEEMING
F. FOREBODING
G. ASININE
H. ECHELON
I. PREMONITIONS
J. PRODIGAL
K. SIEGE
L. PENANCE
M. NONCHALANTLY
N. ARTICULATE
O. CONCEIVE
P. AFFIDAVIT

1. Imagine; form an idea of
2. Unending
3. Wastefully extravagant
4. Full of things; swarming
5. Advance warnings of the future
6. Strong feeling of coming misfortune or evil
7. Written statement or declaration made under oath
8. To have complete possession of; to dominate
9. Level of command, authority, or rank
10. Assault; attack
11. Lengthy, formal speech or writing about a particular topic
12. Distinct, fluent, meaningful, and clear in the power of speech
13. Smothering or suffocating
14. In a way cooly unconcerned, indifferent, or casual
15. Foolish; silly; stupid
16. Act of devotion to pay for a sin or wrongdoing

A=11	B=13	C=8	D=2
E=4	F=6	G=15	H=9
I=5	J=3	K=10	L=16
M=14	N=12	O=1	P=7

Go Ask Alice Vocabulary Word Search 1

```
S N O I T I N O M E R P P R Y I N G J Z
G I F R O I R E F N I V E G A T V X Z B
N N D I X W V N H I Z F R N R C A R D M
I T N L R F T T P N R C I T F C S V K
V E O F E M R G N I M E E T S P I G C W
A R N O C D A S M S L N P U A E L N M C
R M C R R C N M C A T O T C G N L I K M
T I H E I O S L E I X I I E N A A L R R
D N A B M N G N T N C T V S O N T F V N
T A L O I C R Y A P T N E R I C I I H N
T B A D N E E S T R F E C E T E N T V B
K L N I A I S U I O Y T X P A C G S D M
N E T N T V S O V D M N R K T H V M I V
X R L G I E I R A I Q O W D R E X T S P
P J Y B O N O E D G K C T L E L N N C G
N H M J N F N H I A Q M K J S O Y N R C
S M E N S K S C F L Y R U L S N I B E F
Z C Y N P D Q E F K R Y N N I A Y L E D
T S N W O G F L A M E N T E D R W A T W
L X Y F T M C L O D D Y J S A A V S Z W
N O I T A L E V E R Q B I E T R N E R R
E V I T C I D N I V X D L V Y W W E L V
Z T D V Z D Y D A E L B A N G E R P M I
```

Accusations in response to accusations from someone else (14)
Act of devotion to pay for a sin or wrongdoing (7)
Advance warnings of the future (12)
Assault; attack (5)
Blurred from sleep or fatigue; unclear (6)
Bored with life or unimpressed (5)
Common; dull; boring; unimaginative (7)
Disagreement; point of disagreement (10)
Edged or moved up sideways (6)
Expressed grief or regret; mourned (8)
Foolish; silly; stupid (7)
Full of things; swarming (7)
Imagine; form an idea of (8)
In a way cooly unconcerned, indifferent, or casual (12)
Indecisive; unsteady; wavering (11)
Informer, spy, or someone who squeals (4)
Lengthy, formal speech or writing about a particular topic (12)
Level of command, authority, or rank (7)
Looking at closely or curiously (6)
Lower in position, rank, or worth (8)
Not any; no; never (4)
Off or away from the correct or right path (6)

Pursuing with harassment; annoying persistently (11)
Revengeful; with the desire to hurt another (10)
Showing wise self-restraint in behavior (8)
Smothering or suffocating (8)
Something that exists as its own self or being (6)
Something that is remarkable, impressive, or extraordinary (9)
Something that is uncovered, not previously known (10)
Strong feeling of coming misfortune or evil (10)
Stupid or of lesser dignity or value (6)
Suggestive; lustful (9)
The expanse of the sky (9)
The feeling that someone or something is unworthy of one's consideration or respect (7)
Unable to be captured, overthrown, or broken into (11)
Understanding with insight or intuition (10)
Unending (12)
Violations of laws or duties (14)
Wastefully extravagant (8)
Wild, delirious, or frenzied talking (7)
Written statement or declaration made under oath (9)

Go Ask Alice Vocabulary Word Search 1 Answer Key

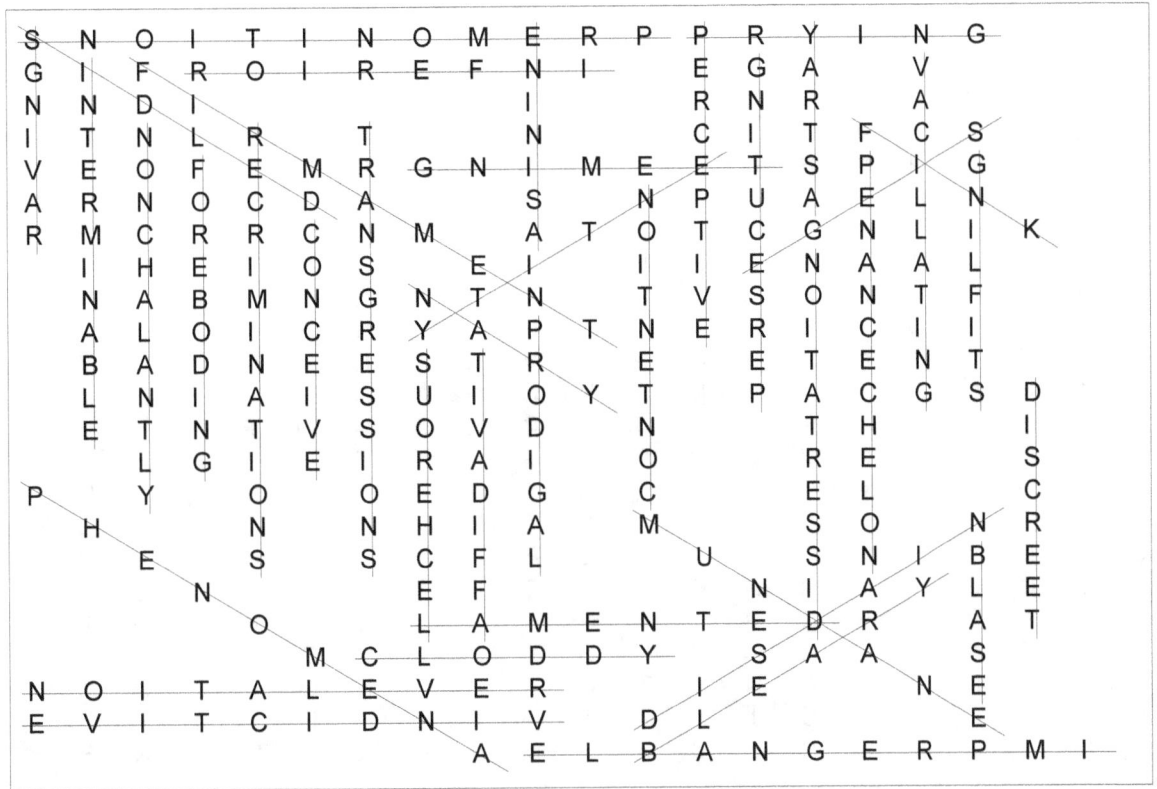

Accusations in response to accusations from someone else (14)
Act of devotion to pay for a sin or wrongdoing (7)
Advance warnings of the future (12)
Assault; attack (5)
Blurred from sleep or fatigue; unclear (6)
Bored with life or unimpressed (5)
Common; dull; boring; unimaginative (7)
Disagreement; point of disagreement (10)
Edged or moved up sideways (6)
Expressed grief or regret; mourned (8)
Foolish; silly; stupid (7)
Full of things; swarming (7)
Imagine; form an idea of (8)
In a way cooly unconcerned, indifferent, or casual (12)
Indecisive; unsteady; wavering (11)
Informer, spy, or someone who squeals (4)
Lengthy, formal speech or writing about a particular topic (12)
Level of command, authority, or rank (7)
Looking at closely or curiously (6)
Lower in position, rank, or worth (8)
Not any; no; never (4)
Off or away from the correct or right path (6)

Pursuing with harassment; annoying persistently (11)
Revengeful; with the desire to hurt another (10)
Showing wise self-restraint in behavior (8)
Smothering or suffocating (8)
Something that exists as its own self or being (6)
Something that is remarkable, impressive, or extraordinary (9)
Something that is uncovered, not previously known (10)
Strong feeling of coming misfortune or evil (10)
Stupid or of lesser dignity or value (6)
Suggestive; lustful (9)
The expanse of the sky (9)
The feeling that someone or something is unworthy of one's consideration or respect (7)
Unable to be captured, overthrown, or broken into (11)
Understanding with insight or intuition (10)
Unending (12)
Violations of laws or duties (14)
Wastefully extravagant (8)
Wild, delirious, or frenzied talking (7)
Written statement or declaration made under oath (9)

Go Ask Alice Vocabulary Word Search 2

```
S N Q Y J E V W E C K V P W D G Y F H H
U V M C V L R C Q V L V R T N S T F Y X
O X H Z F B N Y Q K K O O I E K T A T H
R E V E L A T I O N Y S D B L E A R Y D
E I H P N N S N S T L O I D D L M T M K
H N D E A I Q I I I B W G E Y B V I O N
C S P F R M D T N E E E A C P A A C N P
E C R I Y R N I R I V G L H E N C U O G
L R Y N H E Q O S I N K E E R G I L P W
L I I K Q T F V T T S E E L S E L A O Y
I P N C Y N Y P E G I V R O E R L T L Y
N T G O P I E E N P I N H N C P A E I J
F I Y N N C R I F T T D C J U M T A Z B
E O F C R C V C C O N S C T T I I F E P
R N Q E S A H I D O R T Q M I B N F T K
I A P I R G D A I I N T M P N O G I X C
O S D V G N D T L H S E I X G C N D G B
R T L E I D N D E A N D E T N E M A L M
M R T V L E E S J A N H A L U N X V G T
V A C M T L A Q D N Q T J I C D P I L F
D Y M N D L S N S T I F L I N G E T L X
S M O I B J U J Z Z Z Q T Y G F T J T T
C C S B F M R E C R I M I N A T I O N S
```

Accusations in response to accusations from someone else (14)
Act of devotion to pay for a sin or wrongdoing (7)
Assault; attack (5)
Blurred from sleep or fatigue; unclear (6)
Bored with life or unimpressed (5)
Common; dull; boring; unimaginative (7)
Disagreement; point of disagreement (10)
Distinct, fluent, meaningful, and clear in the power of speech (10)
Edged or moved up sideways (6)
Expressed grief or regret; mourned (8)
Foolish; silly; stupid (7)
Full of things; swarming (7)
Imagine; form an idea of (8)
In a way cooly unconcerned, indifferent, or casual (12)
Indecisive; unsteady; wavering (11)
Informer, spy, or someone who squeals (4)
Level of command, authority, or rank (7)
Looking at closely or curiously (6)
Lower in position, rank, or worth (8)
Marking of words or a message on an item (11)
Mental and emotional strength in facing difficulty (9)

Not any; no; never (4)
Off or away from the correct or right path (6)
Pursuing with harassment; annoying persistently (11)
Recognizing or distinguishing differences (11)
Revengeful; with the desire to hurt another (10)
Showing wise self-restraint in behavior (8)
Smothering or suffocating (8)
Something that exists as its own self or being (6)
Something that is uncovered, not previously known (10)
Strong feeling of coming misfortune or evil (10)
Stupid or of lesser dignity or value (6)
Suggestive; lustful (9)
The feeling that someone or something is unworthy of one's consideration or respect (7)
To have complete possession of; to dominate (10)
Unable to be captured, overthrown, or broken into (11)
Understanding with insight or intuition (10)
Unending (12)
Wastefully extravagant (8)
Wild, delirious, or frenzied talking (7)
Written statement or declaration made under oath (9)

Go Ask Alice Vocabulary Word Search 2 Answer Key

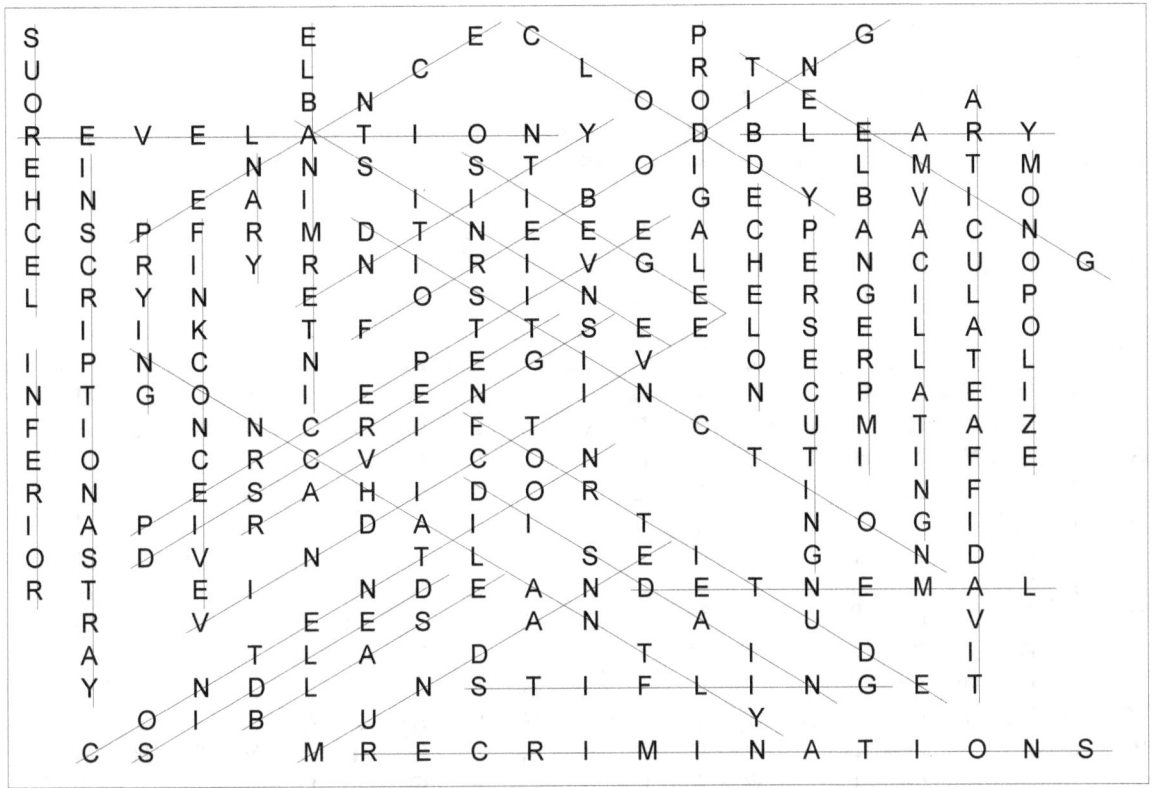

Accusations in response to accusations from someone else (14)
Act of devotion to pay for a sin or wrongdoing (7)
Assault; attack (5)
Blurred from sleep or fatigue; unclear (6)
Bored with life or unimpressed (5)
Common; dull; boring; unimaginative (7)
Disagreement; point of disagreement (10)
Distinct, fluent, meaningful, and clear in the power of speech (10)
Edged or moved up sideways (6)
Expressed grief or regret; mourned (8)
Foolish; silly; stupid (7)
Full of things; swarming (7)
Imagine; form an idea of (8)
In a way cooly unconcerned, indifferent, or casual (12)
Indecisive; unsteady; wavering (11)
Informer, spy, or someone who squeals (4)
Level of command, authority, or rank (7)
Looking at closely or curiously (6)
Lower in position, rank, or worth (8)
Marking of words or a message on an item (11)
Mental and emotional strength in facing difficulty (9)

Not any; no; never (4)
Off or away from the correct or right path (6)
Pursuing with harassment; annoying persistently (11)
Recognizing or distinguishing differences (11)
Revengeful; with the desire to hurt another (10)
Showing wise self-restraint in behavior (8)
Smothering or suffocating (8)
Something that exists as its own self or being (6)
Something that is uncovered, not previously known (10)
Strong feeling of coming misfortune or evil (10)
Stupid or of lesser dignity or value (6)
Suggestive; lustful (9)
The feeling that someone or something is unworthy of one's consideration or respect (7)
To have complete possession of; to dominate (10)
Unable to be captured, overthrown, or broken into (11)
Understanding with insight or intuition (10)
Unending (12)
Wastefully extravagant (8)
Wild, delirious, or frenzied talking (7)
Written statement or declaration made under oath (9)

Go Ask Alice Vocabulary Word Search 3

```
I C O N T E N T I O N L M C D I G V R W
M Q P T I N S C R I P T I O N D N T A Z
P F R L R F Q Y H M F E K T Q V I T V R
R O E A Y A H D U M I E Z S I T E I N N
E R M M Y X N N F D R F S T N U C N G G
G E O E H K D S T P M C N I D C H G H H
N B N N G A N J G I A S N O F I E E S G
A O I T N N Y S N R M I C I L C S L J V
B D T E P E N A N C E D U T I T R O F A
L I I D S T B P F T N S I A N I E N L L
E N O D I L K Z A C T V S N G V P R E T
V G N V E F Y R A N A E C I P E T L N N
A P S A G I E Y R D V N L M O S M V C A
S Q R N E N M R I I Z T O I A N I M H L
I Y G G E K L F E Z K I D R G T S O E A
N H M G K W F C T V B T D C P D J N R H
I D E J D A N N A V E Y Y E S E K O O C
N X X D X O X N L X T L C R S I H P U N
E Q X D C S I V U P E R A A C C D O S O
N D B J Z A Q W C T E X L T K X Y L K N
T X L W D D N T I P M B Y F I X D I E L
M Z P S D F R J T N I V Q R C O N Z L D
W D I Z G N I Y R P N A N E M O N E H P
M D P R O D I G A L G R E G A R I O U S
```

AFFIDAVIT	DISDAIN	LAMENTED	PRODIGAL
ARTICULATE	ECHELON	LECHEROUS	PRYING
ASININE	ENTITY	MONOPOLIZE	RAVINGS
ASTRAY	FINK	MUNDANE	RECRIMINATIONS
BLASE	FIRMAMENT	NARY	REVELATION
BLEARY	FOREBODING	NONCHALANTLY	SIDLED
CLODDY	FORTITUDE	PENANCE	SIEGE
CONCEIVE	GREGARIOUS	PERCEPTIVE	STIFLING
CONTENTION	IMPREGNABLE	PERSECUTING	TEEMING
DEGENERATE	INSCRIPTION	PHENOMENA	TRANSGRESSIONS
DISCREET	INTERMINABLE	PREMONITIONS	VINDICTIVE

Go Ask Alice Vocabulary Word Search 3 Answer Key

AFFIDAVIT	DISDAIN	LAMENTED	PRODIGAL
ARTICULATE	ECHELON	LECHEROUS	PRYING
ASININE	ENTITY	MONOPOLIZE	RAVINGS
ASTRAY	FINK	MUNDANE	RECRIMINATIONS
BLASE	FIRMAMENT	NARY	REVELATION
BLEARY	FOREBODING	NONCHALANTLY	SIDLED
CLODDY	FORTITUDE	PENANCE	SIEGE
CONCEIVE	GREGARIOUS	PERCEPTIVE	STIFLING
CONTENTION	IMPREGNABLE	PERSECUTING	TEEMING
DEGENERATE	INSCRIPTION	PHENOMENA	TRANSGRESSIONS
DISCREET	INTERMINABLE	PREMONITIONS	VINDICTIVE

Go Ask Alice Vocabulary Word Search 4

```
V A C I L L A T I N G N I M E E T C F X
D P L N G N I D O B E R O F S N Y R O S
I E O S X H B X L N X N G N E Y A N C T
S N D C W H V A N Y O E S M M G N C T S
T A D R D D M I R P N M A I N Y S E T D
I N Y I S E A A O A P M P I D V G I T W
N C G P N D E L D V R K L A P L R U T K
C E C T S L I N I Y F A S R L E E D J V
T M E I B Z U N F N I I S I E Q S D E F
I D D O E M D B C T N N T N M J S X J L
O A B N E I N F S F G F R I O H I N N R
N S R S C O M X Q K Z E A N N H O O X V
K R A T L X A P G Q V R Y E I Z N I P T
D L I E I N T F R J L I H J T S S T P J
B V H C S C R F F E S O D Y I U T A R D
E C A X G E U X B I G R Y M O O H L O Y
E F N D N N S L W V D N D C N R X E D J
C D E H I T X L A C Y A A I S E M V I R
L L M H V I F N M T N N V B S H W E G K
S O G A T B Q Z N E S V I L C G R A Z
Y V N A R Y D E G E N E R A T E R K L Y
V T E L B A N I M R E T N I I L N E Q D
H Y H G R E G A R I O U S P I X Z E N
M L P E R S E C U T I N G K F K X S W T
```

AFFIDAVIT	DISTINCTION	INTERMINABLE	PRYING
ARTICULATE	ECHELON	LAMENTED	RAVINGS
ASININE	ENTITY	LECHEROUS	REVELATION
ASTRAY	FINK	MONOPOLIZE	SIDLED
BLASE	FIRMAMENT	MUNDANE	SIEGE
BLEARY	FOREBODING	NARY	STIFLING
CLODDY	FORTITUDE	PENANCE	TEEMING
CONCEIVE	GREGARIOUS	PERSECUTING	TRANSGRESSIONS
DEGENERATE	IMPREGNABLE	PHENOMENA	VACILLATING
DISCREET	INFERIOR	PREMONITIONS	VINDICTIVE
DISDAIN	INSCRIPTION	PRODIGAL	

Go Ask Alice Vocabulary Word Search 4 Answer Key

AFFIDAVIT	DISTINCTION	INTERMINABLE	PRYING
ARTICULATE	ECHELON	LAMENTED	RAVINGS
ASININE	ENTITY	LECHEROUS	REVELATION
ASTRAY	FINK	MONOPOLIZE	SIDLED
BLASE	FIRMAMENT	MUNDANE	SIEGE
BLEARY	FOREBODING	NARY	STIFLING
CLODDY	FORTITUDE	PENANCE	TEEMING
CONCEIVE	GREGARIOUS	PERSECUTING	TRANSGRESSIONS
DEGENERATE	IMPREGNABLE	PHENOMENA	VACILLATING
DISCREET	INFERIOR	PREMONITIONS	VINDICTIVE
DISDAIN	INSCRIPTION	PRODIGAL	

Go Ask Alice Vocabulary Crossword 1

Across
2. Off or away from the correct or right path
4. Wild, delirious, or frenzied talking
6. Something that exists as its own self or being
7. Not any; no; never
8. Informer, spy, or someone who squeals
11. Unending
15. Assault; attack
16. Common; dull; boring; unimaginative
17. The feeling that someone or something is unworthy of one's consideration or respect
18. Level of command, authority, or rank
19. Looking at closely or curiously

Down
1. Act of devotion to pay for a sin or wrongdoing
2. Foolish; silly; stupid
3. Hostile; unfriendly
4. Accusations in response to accusations from someone else
5. Marking of words or a message on an item
9. Pursuing with harassment; annoying persistently
10. Disagreement; point of disagreement
12. Full of things; swarming
13. Something that is uncovered, not previously known
14. Bored with life or unimpressed

Go Ask Alice Vocabulary Crossword 1 Answer Key

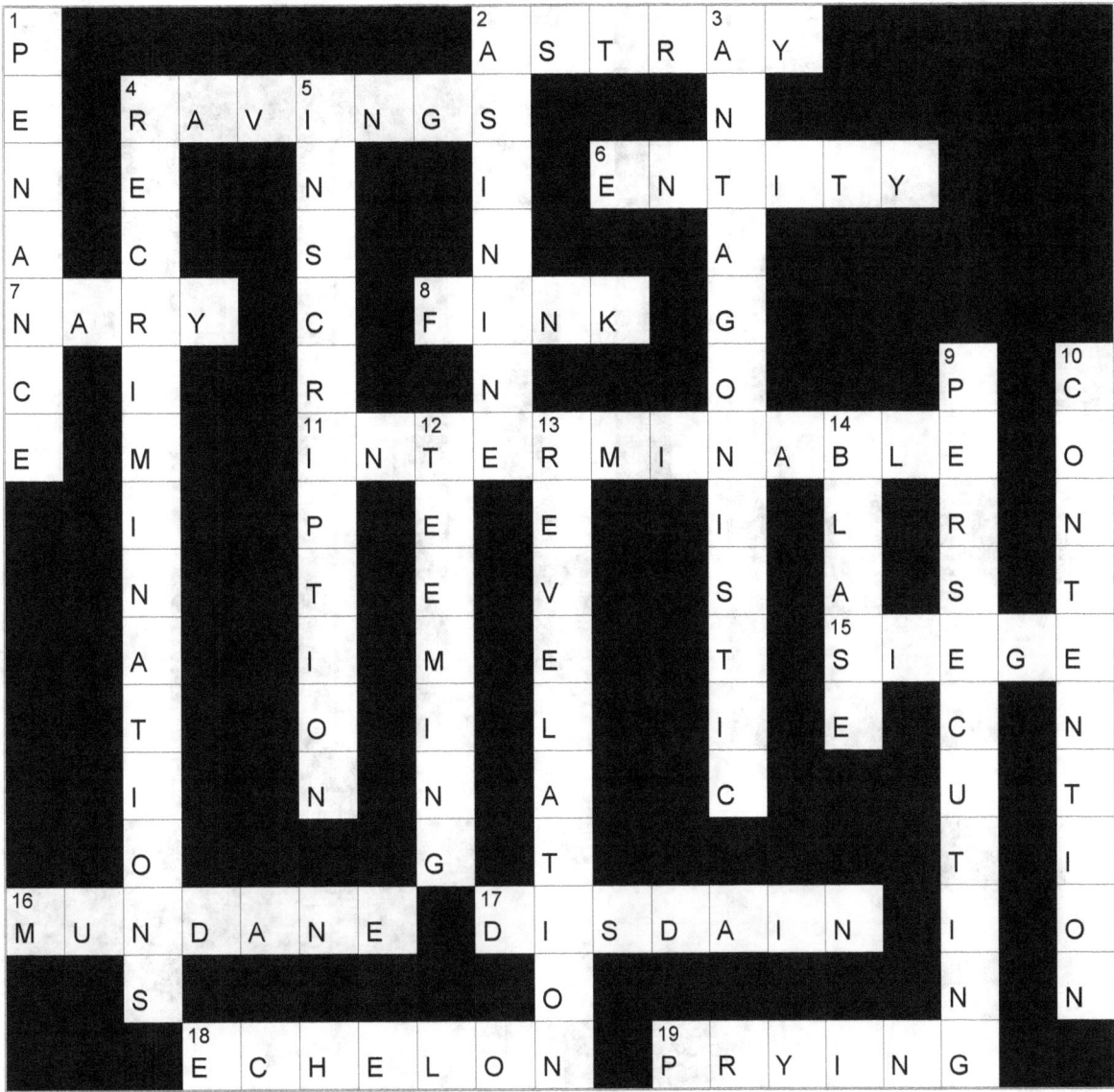

Across
2. Off or away from the correct or right path
4. Wild, delirious, or frenzied talking
6. Something that exists as its own self or being
7. Not any; no; never
8. Informer, spy, or someone who squeals
11. Unending
15. Assault; attack
16. Common; dull; boring; unimaginative
17. The feeling that someone or something is unworthy of one's consideration or respect
18. Level of command, authority, or rank
19. Looking at closely or curiously

Down
1. Act of devotion to pay for a sin or wrongdoing
2. Foolish; silly; stupid
3. Hostile; unfriendly
4. Accusations in response to accusations from someone else
5. Marking of words or a message on an item
9. Pursuing with harassment; annoying persistently
10. Disagreement; point of disagreement
12. Full of things; swarming
13. Something that is uncovered, not previously known
14. Bored with life or unimpressed

Go Ask Alice Vocabulary Crossword 2

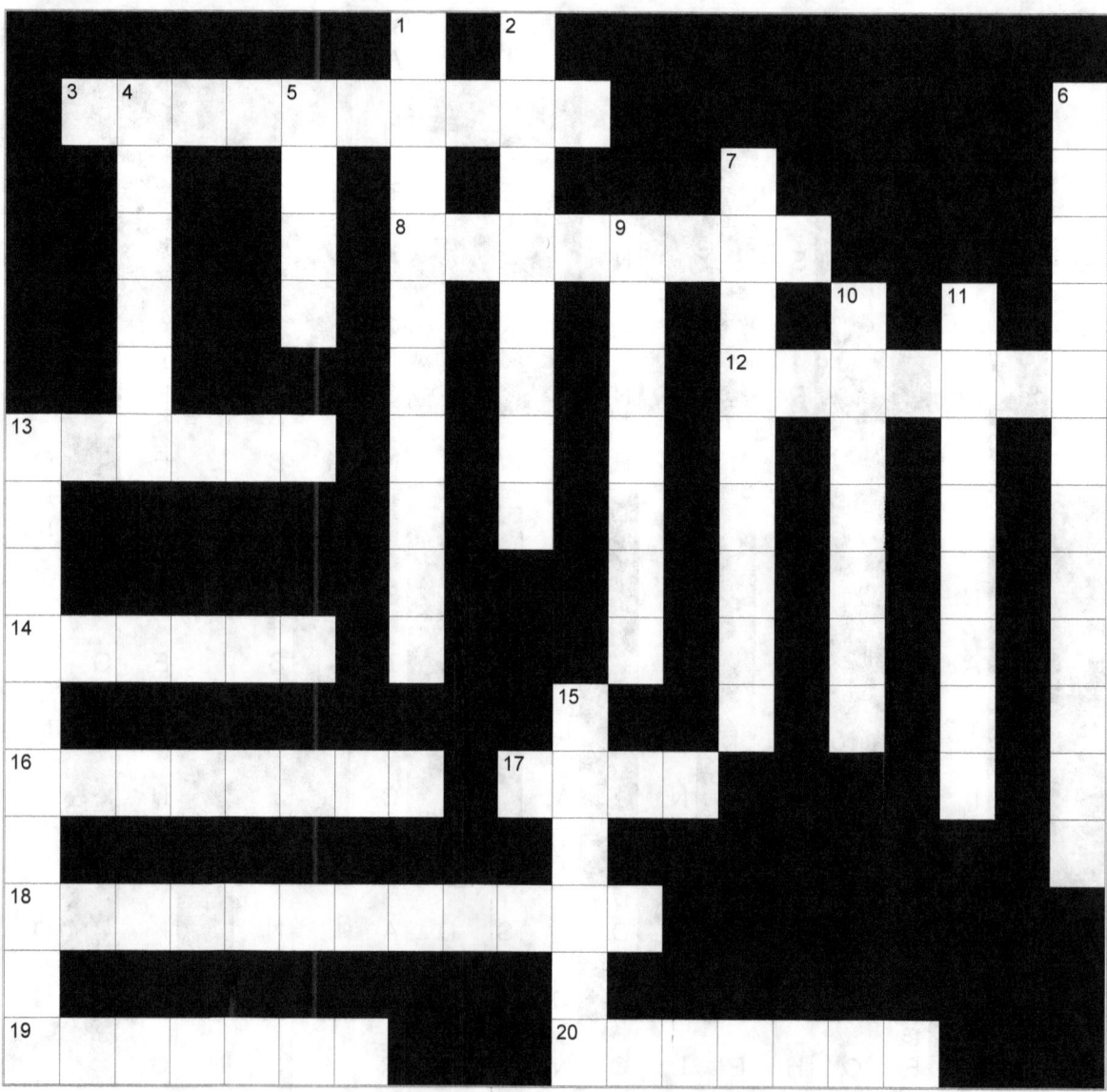

Across

3. One who falls below the desirable level of quality
8. Lower in position, rank, or worth
12. Full of things; swarming
13. Looking at closely or curiously
14. Stupid or of lesser dignity or value
16. Wastefully extravagant
17. Informer, spy, or someone who squeals
18. Unending
19. Level of command, authority, or rank
20. The feeling that someone or something is unworthy of one's consideration or respect

Down

1. Distinct, fluent, meaningful, and clear in the power of speech
2. Smothering or suffocating
4. Something that exists as its own self or being
5. Not any; no; never
6. Hostile; unfriendly
7. Mental and emotional strength in facing difficulty
9. Wild, delirious, or frenzied talking
10. Act of devotion to pay for a sin or wrongdoing
11. Showing wise self-restraint in behavior
13. Understanding with insight or intuition
15. Edged or moved up sideways

Go Ask Alice Vocabulary Crossword 2 Answer Key

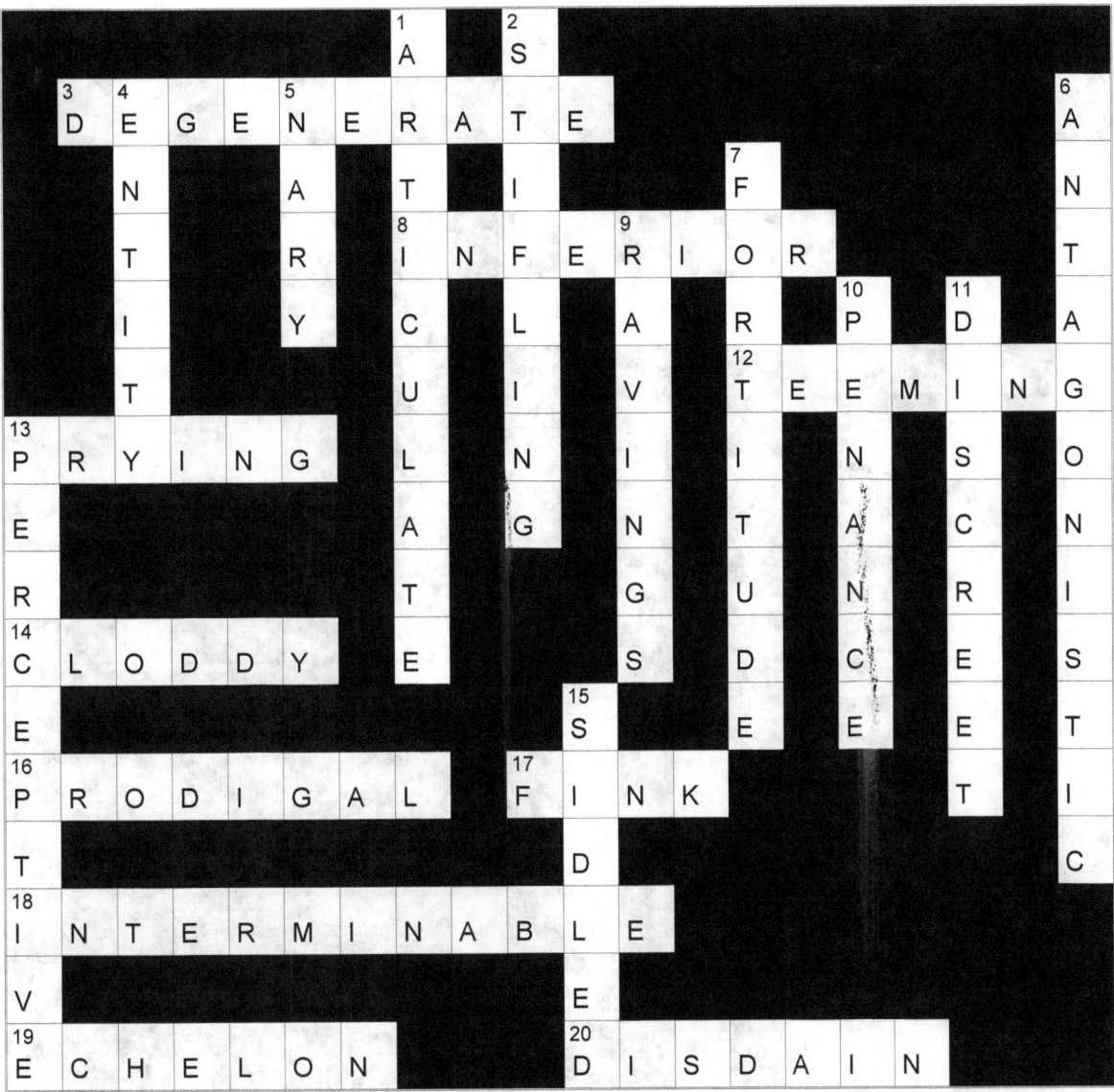

Across
- 3. One who falls below the desirable level of quality
- 8. Lower in position, rank, or worth
- 12. Full of things; swarming
- 13. Looking at closely or curiously
- 14. Stupid or of lesser dignity or value
- 16. Wastefully extravagant
- 17. Informer, spy, or someone who squeals
- 18. Unending
- 19. Level of command, authority, or rank
- 20. The feeling that someone or something is unworthy of one's consideration or respect

Down
- 1. Distinct, fluent, meaningful, and clear in the power of speech
- 2. Smothering or suffocating
- 4. Something that exists as its own self or being
- 5. Not any; no; never
- 6. Hostile; unfriendly
- 7. Mental and emotional strength in facing difficulty
- 9. Wild, delirious, or frenzied talking
- 10. Act of devotion to pay for a sin or wrongdoing
- 11. Showing wise self-restraint in behavior
- 13. Understanding with insight or intuition
- 15. Edged or moved up sideways

Go Ask Alice Vocabulary Crossword 3

Across
1. Wastefully extravagant
2. Bored with life or unimpressed
6. Common; dull; boring; unimaginative
7. Revengeful; with the desire to hurt another
9. In a way cooly unconcerned, indifferent, or casual
14. Informer, spy, or someone who squeals
15. Not any; no; never
16. Looking at closely or curiously
17. Expressed grief or regret; mourned
18. Assault; attack
19. Lower in position, rank, or worth
20. Blurred from sleep or fatigue; unclear

Down
1. Act of devotion to pay for a sin or wrongdoing
3. Suggestive; lustful
4. Smothering or suffocating
5. Something that is uncovered, not previously known
6. To have complete possession of; to dominate
8. Unending
10. Distinct, fluent, meaningful, and clear in the power of speech
11. Hostile; unfriendly
12. The expanse of the sky
13. Imagine; form an idea of

Go Ask Alice Vocabulary Crossword 3 Answer Key

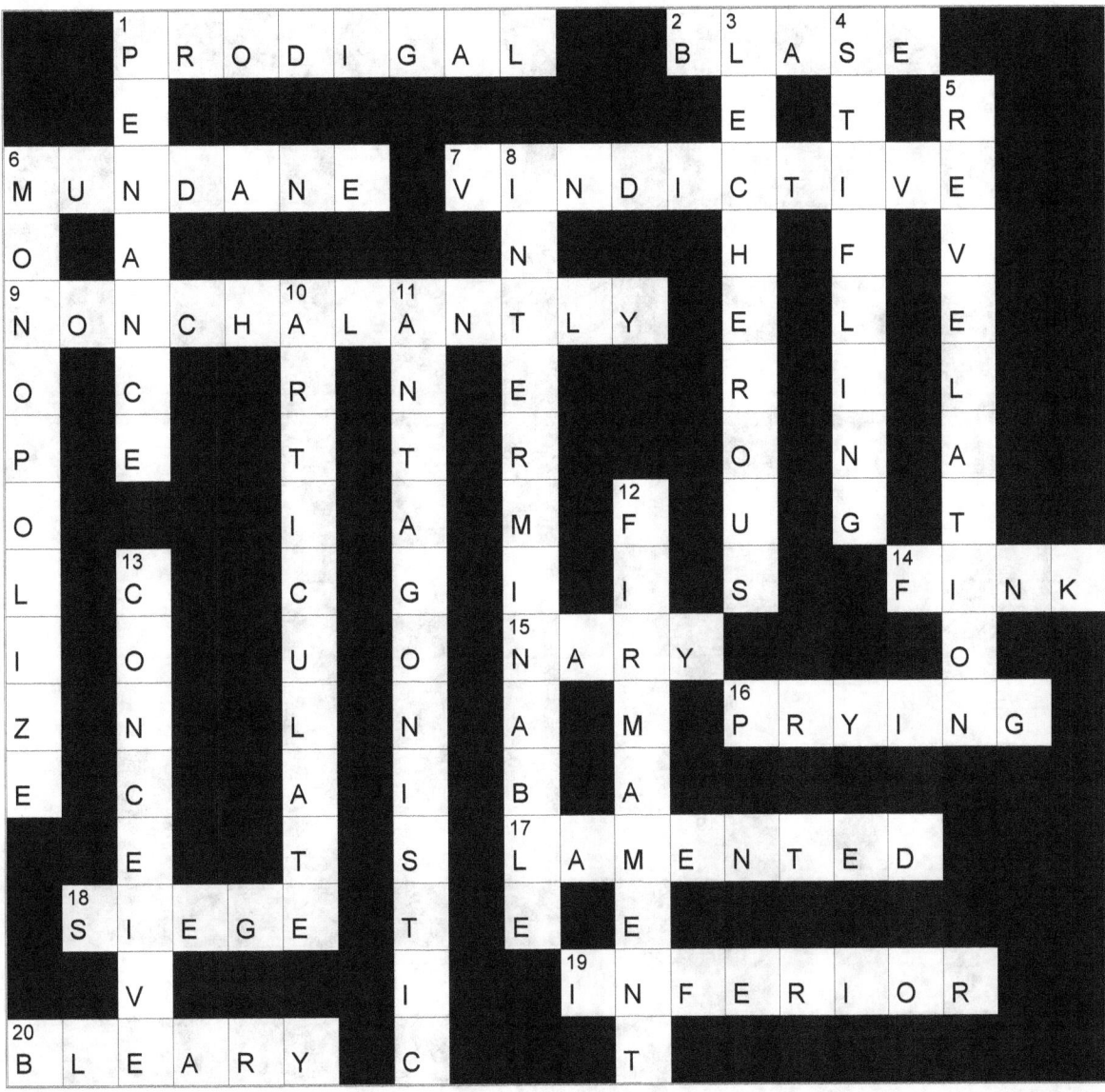

Across
1. Wastefully extravagant
2. Bored with life or unimpressed
6. Common; dull; boring; unimaginative
7. Revengeful; with the desire to hurt another
9. In a way cooly unconcerned, indifferent, or casual
14. Informer, spy, or someone who squeals
15. Not any; no; never
16. Looking at closely or curiously
17. Expressed grief or regret; mourned
18. Assault; attack
19. Lower in position, rank, or worth
20. Blurred from sleep or fatigue; unclear

Down
1. Act of devotion to pay for a sin or wrongdoing
3. Suggestive; lustful
4. Smothering or suffocating
5. Something that is uncovered, not previously known
6. To have complete possession of; to dominate
8. Unending
10. Distinct, fluent, meaningful, and clear in the power of speech
11. Hostile; unfriendly
12. The expanse of the sky
13. Imagine; form an idea of

Go Ask Alice Vocabulary Crossword 4

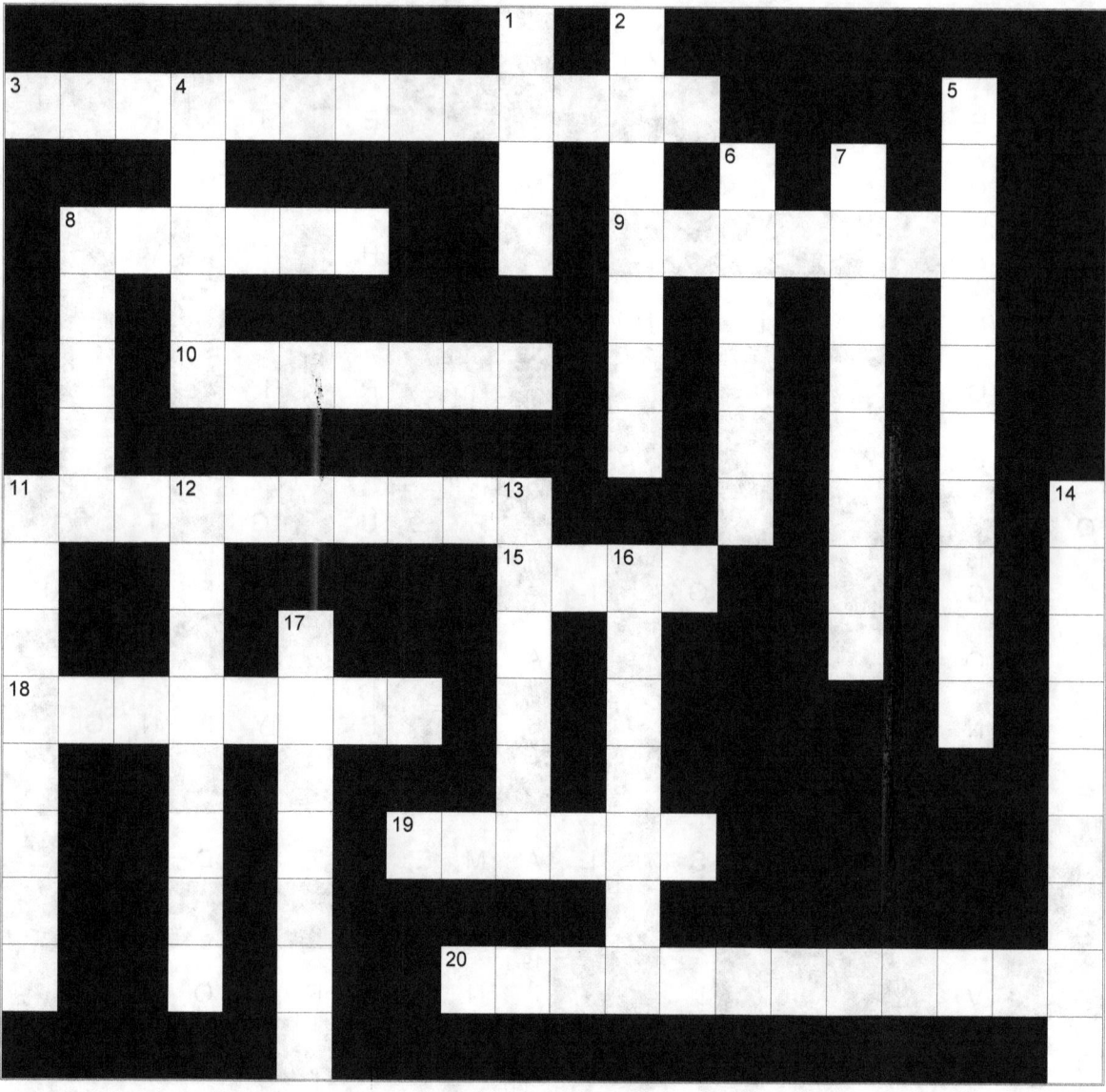

Across

3. Characterized by taking extreme care and/or making great effort
8. Blurred from sleep or fatigue; unclear
9. The feeling that someone or something is unworthy of one's consideration or respect
10. Level of command, authority, or rank
11. Understanding with insight or intuition
15. Not any; no; never
18. Showing wise self-restraint in behavior
19. Looking at closely or curiously
20. Lengthy, formal speech or writing about a particular topic

Down

1. Informer, spy, or someone who squeals
2. Common; dull; boring; unimaginative
4. Assault; attack
5. Disagreement; point of disagreement
6. Off or away from the correct or right path
7. Expressed grief or regret; mourned
8. Bored with life or unimpressed
11. Wastefully extravagant
12. Imagine; form an idea of
13. Something that exists as its own self or being
14. The expanse of the sky
16. Wild, delirious, or frenzied talking
17. Full of things; swarming

Go Ask Alice Vocabulary Crossword 4 Answer Key

Across
3. Characterized by taking extreme care and/or making great effort
8. Blurred from sleep or fatigue; unclear
9. The feeling that someone or something is unworthy of one's consideration or respect
10. Level of command, authority, or rank
11. Understanding with insight or intuition
15. Not any; no; never
18. Showing wise self-restraint in behavior
19. Looking at closely or curiously
20. Lengthy, formal speech or writing about a particular topic

Down
1. Informer, spy, or someone who squeals
2. Common; dull; boring; unimaginative
4. Assault; attack
5. Disagreement; point of disagreement
6. Off or away from the correct or right path
7. Expressed grief or regret; mourned
8. Bored with life or unimpressed
11. Wastefully extravagant
12. Imagine; form an idea of
13. Something that exists as its own self or being
14. The expanse of the sky
16. Wild, delirious, or frenzied talking
17. Full of things; swarming

Go Ask Alice Vocabulary Juggle Letters 1

1. FAFDITAIV = 1. _____
Written statement or declaration made under oath

2. SSSRGONTESRINA = 2. _____
Violations of laws or duties

3. IPGRYN = 3. _____
Looking at closely or curiously

4. PIICITNRNOS = 4. _____
Marking of words or a message on an item

5. RIPTVECEPE = 5. _____
Understanding with insight or intuition

6. MEARLIGEPBN = 6. _____
Unable to be captured, overthrown, or broken into

7. DIRUEFOTT = 7. _____
Mental and emotional strength in facing difficulty

8. EDNCTIVIVI = 8. _____
Revengeful; with the desire to hurt another

9. NDIIDAS = 9. _____
The feeling that someone or something is unworthy of one's consideration or respect

10. IAIAVLLTNGC =10. _____
Indecisive; unsteady; wavering

11. TEERUNIGCSP =11. _____
Pursuing with harassment; annoying persistently

12. IINTCTDNSIO =12. _____
Recognizing or distinguishing differences

13. CPNENAE =13. _____
Act of devotion to pay for a sin or wrongdoing

14. ZIOPMNEOLO =14. _____
To have complete possession of; to dominate

15. VCINEOEC =15. _____
Imagine; form an idea of

Go Ask Alice Vocabulary Juggle Letters 1 Answer Key

1. FAFDITAIV = 1. AFFIDAVIT
   Written statement or declaration made under oath

2. SSSRGONTESRINA = 2. TRANSGRESSIONS
   Violations of laws or duties

3. IPGRYN = 3. PRYING
   Looking at closely or curiously

4. PIICITNRNOS = 4. INSCRIPTION
   Marking of words or a message on an item

5. RIPTVECEPE = 5. PERCEPTIVE
   Understanding with insight or intuition

6. MEARLIGEPBN = 6. IMPREGNABLE
   Unable to be captured, overthrown, or broken into

7. DIRUEFOTT = 7. FORTITUDE
   Mental and emotional strength in facing difficulty

8. EDNCTIVIVI = 8. VINDICTIVE
   Revengeful; with the desire to hurt another

9. NDIIDAS = 9. DISDAIN
   The feeling that someone or something is unworthy of one's consideration or respect

10. IAIAVLLTNGC =10. VACILLATING
    Indecisive; unsteady; wavering

11. TEERUNIGCSP =11. PERSECUTING
    Pursuing with harassment; annoying persistently

12. IINTCTDNSIO =12. DISTINCTION
    Recognizing or distinguishing differences

13. CPNENAE =13. PENANCE
    Act of devotion to pay for a sin or wrongdoing

14. ZIOPMNEOLO =14. MONOPOLIZE
    To have complete possession of; to dominate

15. VCINEOEC =15. CONCEIVE
    Imagine; form an idea of

Go Ask Alice Vocabulary Juggle Letters 2

1. OCUSLERHE = 1. _____
Suggestive; lustful

2. RAGSNIV = 2. _____
Wild, delirious, or frenzied talking

3. EPENNAC = 3. _____
Act of devotion to pay for a sin or wrongdoing

4. DOUETIFRT = 4. _____
Mental and emotional strength in facing difficulty

5. ATDIFVAFI = 5. _____
Written statement or declaration made under oath

6. EPREIVCEPT = 6. _____
Understanding with insight or intuition

7. IINMRAEITCRNOS = 7. _____
Accusations in response to accusations from someone else

8. EHOAENNMP = 8. _____
Something that is remarkable, impressive, or extraordinary

9. NNOTTNEICO = 9. _____
Disagreement; point of disagreement

10. EIOPZONLOM =10. _____
To have complete possession of; to dominate

11. LDIRPOGA =11. _____
Wastefully extravagant

12. IANISNE =12. _____
Foolish; silly; stupid

13. EGSIE =13. _____
Assault; attack

14. NVDCETVIII =14. _____
Revengeful; with the desire to hurt another

15. RATYAS =15. _____
Off or away from the correct or right path

Go Ask Alice Vocabulary Juggle Letters 2 Answer Key

1. OCUSLERHE = 1. LECHEROUS
   Suggestive; lustful

2. RAGSNIV = 2. RAVINGS
   Wild, delirious, or frenzied talking

3. EPENNAC = 3. PENANCE
   Act of devotion to pay for a sin or wrongdoing

4. DOUETIFRT = 4. FORTITUDE
   Mental and emotional strength in facing difficulty

5. ATDIFVAFI = 5. AFFIDAVIT
   Written statement or declaration made under oath

6. EPREIVCEPT = 6. PERCEPTIVE
   Understanding with insight or intuition

7. IINMRAEITCRNOS = 7. RECRIMINATIONS
   Accusations in response to accusations from someone else

8. EHOAENNMP = 8. PHENOMENA
   Something that is remarkable, impressive, or extraordinary

9. NNOTTNEICO = 9. CONTENTION
   Disagreement; point of disagreement

10. EIOPZONLOM =10. MONOPOLIZE
    To have complete possession of; to dominate

11. LDIRPOGA =11. PRODIGAL
    Wastefully extravagant

12. IANISNE =12. ASININE
    Foolish; silly; stupid

13. EGSIE =13. SIEGE
    Assault; attack

14. NVDCETVIII =14. VINDICTIVE
    Revengeful; with the desire to hurt another

15. RATYAS =15. ASTRAY
    Off or away from the correct or right path

Go Ask Alice Vocabulary Juggle Letters 3

1. ILAUTRTEAC = 1. _____
   Distinct, fluent, meaningful, and clear in the power of speech

2. ACIVILNAGLT = 2. _____
   Indecisive; unsteady; wavering

3. URGSGAERIO = 3. _____
   Seeking the company of others; outgoing and sociable

4. TNLEDAME = 4. _____
   Expressed grief or regret; mourned

5. AYNR = 5. _____
   Not any; no; never

6. TTAISGNINOCA = 6. _____
   Hostile; unfriendly

7. EMILBPGRANE = 7. _____
   Unable to be captured, overthrown, or broken into

8. ICSNROITPNI = 8. _____
   Marking of words or a message on an item

9. ICONSUOINETCS = 9. _____
   Characterized by taking extreme care and/or making great effort

10. FTFIVAIAD = 10. _____
    Written statement or declaration made under oath

11. NLNOLTNCAYHA = 11. _____
    In a way cooly unconcerned, indifferent, or casual

12. NTINOCEONT = 12. _____
    Disagreement; point of disagreement

13. GEISE = 13. _____
    Assault; attack

14. MENTGEI = 14. _____
    Full of things; swarming

15. AISDDNI = 15. _____
    The feeling that someone or something is unworthy of one's consideration or respect

Go Ask Alice Vocabulary Juggle Letters 3 Answer Key

1. ILAUTRTEAC = 1. ARTICULATE
Distinct, fluent, meaningful, and clear in the power of speech

2. ACIVILNAGLT = 2. VACILLATING
Indecisive; unsteady; wavering

3. URGSGAERIO = 3. GREGARIOUS
Seeking the company of others; outgoing and sociable

4. TNLEDAME = 4. LAMENTED
Expressed grief or regret; mourned

5. AYNR = 5. NARY
Not any; no; never

6. TTAISGNINOCA = 6. ANTAGONISTIC
Hostile; unfriendly

7. EMILBPGRANE = 7. IMPREGNABLE
Unable to be captured, overthrown, or broken into

8. ICSNROITPNI = 8. INSCRIPTION
Marking of words or a message on an item

9. ICONSUOINETCS = 9. CONSCIENTIOUS
Characterized by taking extreme care and/or making great effort

10. FTFIVAIAD = 10. AFFIDAVIT
Written statement or declaration made under oath

11. NLNOLTNCAYHA = 11. NONCHALANTLY
In a way cooly unconcerned, indifferent, or casual

12. NTINOCEONT = 12. CONTENTION
Disagreement; point of disagreement

13. GEISE = 13. SIEGE
Assault; attack

14. MENTGEI = 14. TEEMING
Full of things; swarming

15. AISDDNI = 15. DISDAIN
The feeling that someone or something is unworthy of one's consideration or respect

Go Ask Alice Vocabulary Juggle Letters 4

1. ETFRIOUTD = 1. _____
   Mental and emotional strength in facing difficulty

2. AIERBITNEMNL = 2. _____
   Unending

3. VALORTENEI = 3. _____
   Something that is uncovered, not previously known

4. OCENVCIE = 4. _____
   Imagine; form an idea of

5. NNIAIES = 5. _____
   Foolish; silly; stupid

6. MEENTIG = 6. _____
   Full of things; swarming

7. EENUIGCSRTP = 7. _____
   Pursuing with harassment; annoying persistently

8. GTIASNTNCAOI = 8. _____
   Hostile; unfriendly

9. MNAEELTD = 9. _____
   Expressed grief or regret; mourned

10. ITAALCNIGLV =10. _____
    Indecisive; unsteady; wavering

11. TFIIAVFAD =11. _____
    Written statement or declaration made under oath

12. NNCTEOTNOI =12. _____
    Disagreement; point of disagreement

13. NIFOEBGROD =13. _____
    Strong feeling of coming misfortune or evil

14. MPOEENHAN =14. _____
    Something that is remarkable, impressive, or extraordinary

15. GESIE =15. _____
    Assault; attack

Go Ask Alice Vocabulary Juggle Letters 4 Answer Key

1. ETFRIOUTD = 1. FORTITUDE
Mental and emotional strength in facing difficulty

2. AIERBITNEMNL = 2. INTERMINABLE
Unending

3. VALORTENEI = 3. REVELATION
Something that is uncovered, not previously known

4. OCENVCIE = 4. CONCEIVE
Imagine; form an idea of

5. NNIAIES = 5. ASININE
Foolish; silly; stupid

6. MEENTIG = 6. TEEMING
Full of things; swarming

7. EENUIGCSRTP = 7. PERSECUTING
Pursuing with harassment; annoying persistently

8. GTIASNTNCAOI = 8. ANTAGONISTIC
Hostile; unfriendly

9. MNAEELTD = 9. LAMENTED
Expressed grief or regret; mourned

10. ITAALCNIGLV = 10. VACILLATING
Indecisive; unsteady; wavering

11. TFIIAVFAD = 11. AFFIDAVIT
Written statement or declaration made under oath

12. NNCTEOTNOI = 12. CONTENTION
Disagreement; point of disagreement

13. NIFOEBGROD = 13. FOREBODING
Strong feeling of coming misfortune or evil

14. MPOEENHAN = 14. PHENOMENA
Something that is remarkable, impressive, or extraordinary

15. GESIE = 15. SIEGE
Assault; attack

AFFIDAVIT	Written statement or declaration made under oath
ANTAGONISTIC	Hostile; unfriendly
ARTICULATE	Distinct, fluent, meaningful, and clear in the power of speech
ASININE	Foolish; silly; stupid
ASTRAY	Off or away from the correct or right path

BLASE	Bored with life or unimpressed
BLEARY	Blurred from sleep or fatigue; unclear
CLODDY	Stupid or of lesser dignity or value
CONCEIVE	Imagine; form an idea of
CONSCIENTIOUS	Characterized by taking extreme care and/or making great effort

CONTENTION	Disagreement; point of disagreement
DEGENERATE	One who falls below the desirable level of quality
DISCREET	Showing wise self-restraint in behavior
DISDAIN	The feeling that someone or something is unworthy of one's consideration or respect
DISSERTATION	Lengthy, formal speech or writing about a particular topic

DISTINCTION	Recognizing or distinguishing differences
ECHELON	Level of command, authority, or rank
ENTITY	Something that exists as its own self or being
FINK	Informer, spy, or someone who squeals
FIRMAMENT	The expanse of the sky

FOREBODING	Strong feeling of coming misfortune or evil
FORTITUDE	Mental and emotional strength in facing difficulty
GREGARIOUS	Seeking the company of others; outgoing and sociable
IMPREGNABLE	Unable to be captured, overthrown, or broken into
INFERIOR	Lower in position, rank, or worth

INSCRIPTION	Marking of words or a message on an item
INTERMINABLE	Unending
LAMENTED	Expressed grief or regret; mourned
LECHEROUS	Suggestive; lustful
MONOPOLIZE	To have complete possession of; to dominate

MUNDANE	Common; dull; boring; unimaginative
NARY	Not any; no; never
NONCHALANTLY	In a way cooly unconcerned, indifferent, or casual
PENANCE	Act of devotion to pay for a sin or wrongdoing
PERCEPTIVE	Understanding with insight or intuition

PERSECUTING	Pursuing with harassment; annoying persistently
PHENOMENA	Something that is remarkable, impressive, or extraordinary
PREMONITIONS	Advance warnings of the future
PRODIGAL	Wastefully extravagant
PRYING	Looking at closely or curiously

RAVINGS	Wild, delirious, or frenzied talking
RECRIMINATIONS	Accusations in response to accusations from someone else
REVELATION	Something that is uncovered, not previously known
SIDLED	Edged or moved up sideways
SIEGE	Assault; attack

STIFLING	Smothering or suffocating
TEEMING	Full of things; swarming
TRANSGRESSIONS	Violations of laws or duties
VACILLATING	Indecisive; unsteady; wavering
VINDICTIVE	Revengeful; with the desire to hurt another

Go Ask Alice Vocabulary

FINK	VACILLATING	AFFIDAVIT	MUNDANE	INFERIOR
DISTINCTION	TEEMING	PREMONITIONS	SIEGE	VINDICTIVE
STIFLING	ANTAGONISTIC	FREE SPACE	BLASE	PHENOMENA
FOREBODING	PERCEPTIVE	DISDAIN	PRODIGAL	NARY
PENANCE	RECRIMINATIONS	PRYING	CONTENTION	NONCHALANTLY

Go Ask Alice Vocabulary

ECHELON	BLEARY	DEGENERATE	PERSECUTING	LAMENTED
MONOPOLIZE	LECHEROUS	CLODDY	ASTRAY	ARTICULATE
ENTITY	CONSCIENTIOUS	FREE SPACE	DISCREET	CONCEIVE
DISSERTATION	INSCRIPTION	REVELATION	ASININE	INTERMINABLE
SIDLED	FORTITUDE	FIRMAMENT	RAVINGS	NONCHALANTLY

Go Ask Alice Vocabulary

BLASE	CONSCIENTIOUS	RECRIMINATIONS	LECHEROUS	VACILLATING
BLEARY	CONTENTION	AFFIDAVIT	FORTITUDE	SIDLED
DISTINCTION	FOREBODING	FREE SPACE	IMPREGNABLE	PRYING
PERCEPTIVE	TEEMING	INSCRIPTION	STIFLING	VINDICTIVE
ENTITY	GREGARIOUS	MONOPOLIZE	PENANCE	INTERMINABLE

Go Ask Alice Vocabulary

FINK	PERSECUTING	INFERIOR	REVELATION	PHENOMENA
NONCHALANTLY	CONCEIVE	PREMONITIONS	NARY	DISDAIN
ASTRAY	ARTICULATE	FREE SPACE	DEGENERATE	DISCREET
MUNDANE	RAVINGS	DISSERTATION	LAMENTED	ECHELON
CLODDY	FIRMAMENT	PRODIGAL	SIEGE	INTERMINABLE

Go Ask Alice Vocabulary

DEGENERATE	LAMENTED	NONCHALANTLY	AFFIDAVIT	LECHEROUS
CONCEIVE	DISDAIN	CONTENTION	RECRIMINATIONS	PRODIGAL
PHENOMENA	SIDLED	FREE SPACE	REVELATION	FINK
NARY	INTERMINABLE	DISSERTATION	CONSCIENTIOUS	IMPREGNABLE
BLEARY	FORTITUDE	RAVINGS	ARTICULATE	CLODDY

Go Ask Alice Vocabulary

INSCRIPTION	PENANCE	DISTINCTION	ENTITY	ASININE
FOREBODING	SIEGE	VINDICTIVE	ASTRAY	ANTAGONISTIC
ECHELON	GREGARIOUS	FREE SPACE	TEEMING	PERSECUTING
INFERIOR	FIRMAMENT	STIFLING	PERCEPTIVE	VACILLATING
DISCREET	MUNDANE	BLASE	MONOPOLIZE	CLODDY

Go Ask Alice Vocabulary

PREMONITIONS	ASTRAY	MUNDANE	DISDAIN	RAVINGS
LAMENTED	DEGENERATE	GREGARIOUS	BLASE	ECHELON
CONSCIENTIOUS	NONCHALANTLY	FREE SPACE	PRODIGAL	INSCRIPTION
SIEGE	BLEARY	MONOPOLIZE	PERSECUTING	VINDICTIVE
INTERMINABLE	DISCREET	FOREBODING	FORTITUDE	PENANCE

Go Ask Alice Vocabulary

CONTENTION	IMPREGNABLE	AFFIDAVIT	STIFLING	CONCEIVE
FINK	FIRMAMENT	DISTINCTION	DISSERTATION	RECRIMINATIONS
SIDLED	ASININE	FREE SPACE	ENTITY	NARY
VACILLATING	ANTAGONISTIC	PHENOMENA	PRYING	CLODDY
REVELATION	LECHEROUS	TEEMING	PERCEPTIVE	PENANCE

Go Ask Alice Vocabulary

PREMONITIONS	DEGENERATE	INTERMINABLE	SIEGE	REVELATION
ANTAGONISTIC	ECHELON	INSCRIPTION	RECRIMINATIONS	MONOPOLIZE
MUNDANE	PERSECUTING	FREE SPACE	DISDAIN	FIRMAMENT
AFFIDAVIT	DISTINCTION	TEEMING	LAMENTED	CONTENTION
DISCREET	ASTRAY	PRODIGAL	PHENOMENA	VINDICTIVE

Go Ask Alice Vocabulary

ASININE	PENANCE	CONSCIENTIOUS	VACILLATING	NONCHALANTLY
CLODDY	FORTITUDE	GREGARIOUS	SIDLED	PERCEPTIVE
IMPREGNABLE	ENTITY	FREE SPACE	NARY	STIFLING
ARTICULATE	FOREBODING	LECHEROUS	CONCEIVE	PRYING
DISSERTATION	FINK	INFERIOR	BLEARY	VINDICTIVE

Go Ask Alice Vocabulary

PERSECUTING	PRYING	FORTITUDE	STIFLING	SIDLED
INTERMINABLE	LECHEROUS	ARTICULATE	VINDICTIVE	SIEGE
ANTAGONISTIC	RAVINGS	FREE SPACE	NARY	BLEARY
TEEMING	CONTENTION	NONCHALANTLY	CONSCIENTIOUS	PHENOMENA
PRODIGAL	ECHELON	MONOPOLIZE	RECRIMINATIONS	REVELATION

Go Ask Alice Vocabulary

PREMONITIONS	DISCREET	PERCEPTIVE	FIRMAMENT	DISTINCTION
DISSERTATION	AFFIDAVIT	CONCEIVE	MUNDANE	INFERIOR
LAMENTED	DISDAIN	FREE SPACE	FINK	PENANCE
GREGARIOUS	INSCRIPTION	BLASE	FOREBODING	IMPREGNABLE
DEGENERATE	ENTITY	VACILLATING	ASTRAY	REVELATION

Go Ask Alice Vocabulary

FINK	DISDAIN	CONSCIENTIOUS	DISTINCTION	IMPREGNABLE
PRODIGAL	SIDLED	PHENOMENA	FOREBODING	ASININE
REVELATION	DISSERTATION	FREE SPACE	INSCRIPTION	FORTITUDE
DEGENERATE	AFFIDAVIT	VINDICTIVE	LECHEROUS	FIRMAMENT
CONTENTION	ANTAGONISTIC	TEEMING	SIEGE	NONCHALANTLY

Go Ask Alice Vocabulary

MUNDANE	CLODDY	INTERMINABLE	ECHELON	PRYING
NARY	RAVINGS	ARTICULATE	PENANCE	ENTITY
DISCREET	RECRIMINATIONS	FREE SPACE	STIFLING	PREMONITIONS
BLASE	ASTRAY	VACILLATING	PERSECUTING	CONCEIVE
GREGARIOUS	LAMENTED	INFERIOR	MONOPOLIZE	NONCHALANTLY

Go Ask Alice Vocabulary

ASTRAY	REVELATION	PRODIGAL	RAVINGS	FINK
AFFIDAVIT	ENTITY	DISSERTATION	LAMENTED	ANTAGONISTIC
GREGARIOUS	FIRMAMENT	FREE SPACE	VACILLATING	PRYING
PERCEPTIVE	CONTENTION	BLEARY	DEGENERATE	BLASE
CLODDY	INTERMINABLE	DISTINCTION	PENANCE	ARTICULATE

Go Ask Alice Vocabulary

PHENOMENA	PREMONITIONS	SIEGE	ECHELON	FOREBODING
STIFLING	INFERIOR	DISCREET	ASININE	MONOPOLIZE
MUNDANE	LECHEROUS	FREE SPACE	SIDLED	NARY
IMPREGNABLE	PERSECUTING	INSCRIPTION	NONCHALANTLY	TEEMING
FORTITUDE	RECRIMINATIONS	DISDAIN	CONSCIENTIOUS	ARTICULATE

Go Ask Alice Vocabulary

DEGENERATE	DISTINCTION	CONTENTION	DISDAIN	LAMENTED
VACILLATING	MUNDANE	PERSECUTING	INTERMINABLE	CONSCIENTIOUS
SIEGE	TEEMING	FREE SPACE	AFFIDAVIT	LECHEROUS
FOREBODING	FORTITUDE	GREGARIOUS	REVELATION	RAVINGS
BLASE	DISSERTATION	ENTITY	VINDICTIVE	PREMONITIONS

Go Ask Alice Vocabulary

ANTAGONISTIC	ARTICULATE	CONCEIVE	PENANCE	STIFLING
CLODDY	INSCRIPTION	PRYING	DISCREET	NARY
MONOPOLIZE	FINK	FREE SPACE	PHENOMENA	BLEARY
PRODIGAL	ASININE	ECHELON	FIRMAMENT	ASTRAY
SIDLED	RECRIMINATIONS	IMPREGNABLE	NONCHALANTLY	PREMONITIONS

Go Ask Alice Vocabulary

CONCEIVE	BLEARY	INFERIOR	INTERMINABLE	NARY
STIFLING	MUNDANE	CONTENTION	DISSERTATION	PRODIGAL
RAVINGS	NONCHALANTLY	FREE SPACE	PREMONITIONS	LAMENTED
MONOPOLIZE	SIDLED	RECRIMINATIONS	SIEGE	LECHEROUS
PHENOMENA	ASTRAY	IMPREGNABLE	ARTICULATE	INSCRIPTION

Go Ask Alice Vocabulary

ANTAGONISTIC	CONSCIENTIOUS	FIRMAMENT	FOREBODING	BLASE
GREGARIOUS	DISTINCTION	PERCEPTIVE	PENANCE	VINDICTIVE
DEGENERATE	DISDAIN	FREE SPACE	FINK	AFFIDAVIT
PRYING	VACILLATING	PERSECUTING	ECHELON	TEEMING
DISCREET	ASININE	REVELATION	ENTITY	INSCRIPTION

Go Ask Alice Vocabulary

DISSERTATION	STIFLING	CLODDY	AFFIDAVIT	DISTINCTION
ASTRAY	PRYING	LAMENTED	ASININE	MONOPOLIZE
FORTITUDE	VACILLATING	FREE SPACE	REVELATION	SIDLED
TEEMING	BLEARY	IMPREGNABLE	RECRIMINATIONS	PREMONITIONS
ARTICULATE	MUNDANE	NARY	ANTAGONISTIC	PHENOMENA

Go Ask Alice Vocabulary

VINDICTIVE	DEGENERATE	PENANCE	FINK	INFERIOR
CONSCIENTIOUS	ECHELON	SIEGE	CONCEIVE	ENTITY
PERSECUTING	PRODIGAL	FREE SPACE	INSCRIPTION	FOREBODING
NONCHALANTLY	INTERMINABLE	GREGARIOUS	DISDAIN	PERCEPTIVE
LECHEROUS	BLASE	CONTENTION	DISCREET	PHENOMENA

Go Ask Alice Vocabulary

DISCREET	VINDICTIVE	ASININE	RECRIMINATIONS	PREMONITIONS
NARY	DISSERTATION	PHENOMENA	CONTENTION	PERCEPTIVE
CONCEIVE	GREGARIOUS	FREE SPACE	INFERIOR	FINK
IMPREGNABLE	SIDLED	ARTICULATE	PRODIGAL	BLEARY
CLODDY	MONOPOLIZE	ENTITY	FOREBODING	LECHEROUS

Go Ask Alice Vocabulary

MUNDANE	FORTITUDE	DISDAIN	FIRMAMENT	RAVINGS
PRYING	INTERMINABLE	VACILLATING	BLASE	NONCHALANTLY
CONSCIENTIOUS	ANTAGONISTIC	FREE SPACE	ECHELON	PERSECUTING
DEGENERATE	TEEMING	STIFLING	REVELATION	SIEGE
INSCRIPTION	AFFIDAVIT	PENANCE	DISTINCTION	LECHEROUS

Go Ask Alice Vocabulary

BLEARY	AFFIDAVIT	PRODIGAL	IMPREGNABLE	RECRIMINATIONS
CONCEIVE	VACILLATING	INTERMINABLE	LECHEROUS	STIFLING
ENTITY	TEEMING	FREE SPACE	CONSCIENTIOUS	ASININE
DISDAIN	INSCRIPTION	REVELATION	CLODDY	PENANCE
VINDICTIVE	ASTRAY	PERCEPTIVE	FIRMAMENT	DISCREET

Go Ask Alice Vocabulary

NONCHALANTLY	DISTINCTION	CONTENTION	NARY	MUNDANE
DEGENERATE	ECHELON	SIDLED	DISSERTATION	PHENOMENA
SIEGE	FOREBODING	FREE SPACE	FINK	INFERIOR
PRYING	GREGARIOUS	FORTITUDE	BLASE	PERSECUTING
PREMONITIONS	ARTICULATE	ANTAGONISTIC	LAMENTED	DISCREET

Go Ask Alice Vocabulary

DISCREET	FIRMAMENT	INTERMINABLE	NARY	PHENOMENA
CLODDY	PRODIGAL	FOREBODING	FORTITUDE	SIDLED
PRYING	NONCHALANTLY	FREE SPACE	SIEGE	REVELATION
GREGARIOUS	PREMONITIONS	CONSCIENTIOUS	INSCRIPTION	BLASE
PERCEPTIVE	RECRIMINATIONS	LECHEROUS	VINDICTIVE	ECHELON

Go Ask Alice Vocabulary

PENANCE	BLEARY	FINK	CONCEIVE	MONOPOLIZE
ENTITY	ANTAGONISTIC	TEEMING	LAMENTED	CONTENTION
STIFLING	MUNDANE	FREE SPACE	DISTINCTION	DISSERTATION
PERSECUTING	DISDAIN	DEGENERATE	ASININE	INFERIOR
ARTICULATE	ASTRAY	VACILLATING	IMPREGNABLE	ECHELON

Go Ask Alice Vocabulary

CLODDY	CONSCIENTIOUS	DEGENERATE	FIRMAMENT	PREMONITIONS
CONTENTION	DISSERTATION	LAMENTED	PERCEPTIVE	BLEARY
CONCEIVE	GREGARIOUS	FREE SPACE	ASTRAY	DISTINCTION
REVELATION	ARTICULATE	DISDAIN	NONCHALANTLY	FOREBODING
SIEGE	INTERMINABLE	BLASE	LECHEROUS	PRODIGAL

Go Ask Alice Vocabulary

MUNDANE	PRYING	ECHELON	DISCREET	PHENOMENA
PERSECUTING	VACILLATING	RAVINGS	FORTITUDE	PENANCE
INSCRIPTION	MONOPOLIZE	FREE SPACE	ENTITY	ASININE
SIDLED	INFERIOR	FINK	IMPREGNABLE	VINDICTIVE
TEEMING	ANTAGONISTIC	NARY	AFFIDAVIT	PRODIGAL

Go Ask Alice Vocabulary

ANTAGONISTIC	FINK	SIEGE	LAMENTED	GREGARIOUS
BLASE	ARTICULATE	STIFLING	VACILLATING	DISCREET
ECHELON	DISTINCTION	FREE SPACE	NONCHALANTLY	FOREBODING
AFFIDAVIT	ASTRAY	PERSECUTING	IMPREGNABLE	DISSERTATION
REVELATION	CLODDY	INSCRIPTION	CONTENTION	PRODIGAL

Go Ask Alice Vocabulary

ENTITY	INFERIOR	MUNDANE	TEEMING	PENANCE
PRYING	VINDICTIVE	SIDLED	RAVINGS	LECHEROUS
PREMONITIONS	ASININE	FREE SPACE	BLEARY	PHENOMENA
PERCEPTIVE	RECRIMINATIONS	CONSCIENTIOUS	INTERMINABLE	FIRMAMENT
CONCEIVE	MONOPOLIZE	FORTITUDE	DISDAIN	PRODIGAL

www.ingramcontent.com/pod-product-compliance
Lightning Source LLC
Chambersburg PA
CBHW081456070526
44586CB00019B/2373